PRAISE FOR TWO CROWNS, ONE KINGDOM

As a mental health counselor, I see most people are desperate for love and connections. Drs. Jake and Jenn have created a must read for all who desire love for a lifetime! *Two Crowns, One Kingdom* joyfully offers practical, step-by-step guidance toward staying in love for the rest of your life. If you want fairytale love, this is the book to read.

—Dr. Cynthia Preszler, MA, LMHC
Director of Counseling Grace Clinic

Drs. Jake and Jennifer Dean-Hill have done a beautiful job of addressing relevant marriage issues in their book, *Two Crowns, One Kingdom*. They offer time-tested principles in an innovative story that will bring you hope and inspiration. They share how they have navigated they're own fairytale journey in an honest and transparent way and give you a unique framework to help you do the same. This book is a must read for any couple at any stage of life, as well as being a great resource for your practice or marriage ministry. Don't give up on your fairytale ending!

—Kristi Haynes
Mental Health Trainer and Marriage Coach

Drs. Jake and Jenn Dean-Hill have perfectly merged their personal relationship experience, years of clinical therapy experience, and proven best practices in their newly released book, *Two Crowns, One Kingdom: Helping Couples Navigate the Dark Forest to Reach Their "Happily Ever After."* The book offers deep learning with practical, proven steps to understanding yourself and understanding your romantic partner. If you invest the time and energy into learning and applying Drs. Jake and Jenn's teachings, you can feel confident that your relationship can not only heal but thrive.

—Dr. Jean M. Ollis, LISW-S, MSW, DMin
Mental Health Therapist
Assistant Professor of Social Work

This is a fresh approach to a timeless story. Drs. Jake and Jenn bring life to well researched concepts, gender differences, and every basic human need—to be loved! *Two Crowns, One Kingdom* provides an imaginative and applicable map to guide the reader through a relationship journey with effective tools to promote equity and acceptance. I appreciate how this book promotes bravery for the reader to self-reflect, lead with vulnerability, and invest in a lasting legacy. Definitely recommending this book to my clients and their loved ones!

—Shawnna Burke, MA, LMFT, PLLC
Marriage & Family Therapist

It has been a great blessing to work with and learn from Drs. Jake and Jenn Dean-Hill. Their professional and educational experience has produced in them a remarkable well of wisdom from which they draw in this book.

—Micah & Sara Riesenweber
Lead Pastors, The Vine Church

The *One Kingdom* video series has proven to be a unique, insightful journey for us. We can't say enough about how incredibly helpful the One Kingdom relationship model is. Couples who want to endure what life presents must invest time and energy to make it work. The One Kingdom series has given us the tools to know how to invest our time and energy and make us successful in the long run. This series was so impressive we felt compelled to host the One Kingdom program for small groups through our local church. We witnessed its impact on a wide range of couples, from those who just recently met to those married for many years. It was an amazing experience to share this program with others and see the positive impacts it had on their relationships. If you desire a happier, healthier, enduring relationship that will carry you through the best and worst of times, this material is a must. We make Purple a priority!

—Curtis & Karen King
One Kingdom video series participants and leaders

TWO CROWNS ONE KINGDOM

A JOURNEY FOR COUPLES

TWO CROWNS ONE KINGDOM

Navigate the dark forest to reach your happily-ever-after

DRS. JAKE AND JENN DEAN-HILL

ILLUMIFY
MEDIA.COM

TWO CROWNS ONE KINGDOM

Published by
Illumify Media Global
www.IllumifyMedia.com
"Let's bring your book to life!"

Library of Congress Control Number: 2022901304

Paperback ISBN: 978-1-955043-08-3

Typeset by Art Innovations (http://artinnovations.in/)
Cover design by Debbie Lewis

Printed in the United States of America

DEDICATION

We dedicate this book to the amazing One Kingdom team, who spent tireless hours making this dream a reality. Thank you, Tyler, Meg, Jeremy, and Elijah—we have such fond memories of the fun and laughter that always accompanied the creative process.

We also dedicate this book to all the couples around the world who are striving to "make purple" together and live their "happily ever after" to the best of their ability.

CONTENTS

ACKNOWLEDGMENTS

We are grateful to the thousands of couples who have walked through the doors of our counseling practice and taught us what real marriage looks like and challenged us to write these materials to make marriages better.

We thank our kids, McKenna and Dawson, for being our biggest fans, cheering us on along the way and putting up with our countless hours of writing and developing.

We also thank both of our parents who modeled longevity in marriage and a beautiful faithfulness to their vows. Through sickness and in health, they showed us what it truly means to love unconditionally.

We thank our own marriage therapists, coaches, and mentors who have helped us walk our journey and have provided us the tools we needed to live our best marriage.

We are grateful for our dear friends who have been vulnerable with their marriage struggles and have taken their marriage vows seriously alongside us. They have been some of our greatest inspirations.

We are forever grateful to Karen at Illumify Media Global for her enormous help skillfully editing and formatting this book to become the amazing work of art it turned out to be.

And none of this would be possible without the incredible love and grace of our Lord and Savior, who showers us with blessings beyond measure!

INTRODUCTION — ONCE UPON A TIME

> *If you want your children to be intelligent, read them fairy tales. If you want them to be more intelligent, read them more fairy tales.*
>
> **—Albert Einstein**

Why do we love fairy tales?

Our society is enamored with fairy tales.

We love the happy endings in which the hero conquers evil, the lovers are reunited, and the impossible becomes possible.

We love the adventure of entering into exciting new worlds where our deepest longings are met and where there is rewarding closure to every story.

Fairy tales bring out the hero in all of us and the child within.

Marriage taps into our longing to experience our own fairy-tale stories, to meet and marry the love of our life, someone who chose us above all others and fulfills our wildest dreams.

We enter marriage believing we are entering into a great adventure in which we are cherished, respected, and admired by someone else.

We are embarking on a storybook life where we get to be the hero and leading lady, prince and princess, king and queen, and rule together happily ever after for the rest of our lives.

If you want proof, consider that Disney has built an entire empire on these ideas. In 2012 Disney grossed over $42 billion primarily on movies and merchandise created around fairy tales. And lest we wonder if girls actually long to be princesses, in 2015 the Disney Princess franchise brought in $2.4 billion, and more than twenty-four million guests of all ages have seen Broadway's version of *Beauty and the Beast.*

By simply feeding our longings for fairy tales, Disney has made a fortune.

Indeed, there is something about fairy tales that seems hardwired into our deepest desires.

Cinderella is the oldest and most told fairy tale in every culture, which means this is a story that touches the hearts of humans around the world. To be discovered, redeemed from the ashes, and promoted to a place of power, prestige, and influence is the heart longing of every human.

We are also moved by the prince's side of the story. Imagine! To search the world relentlessly in search of true love, to look past the soot and ashes bestowed by the world and see the true worth of your beloved, to have your relentless pursuit rewarded with true love and happiness ever after—themes like these move us, man and woman alike.

Who wouldn't want this, regardless of your age, gender, or ethnicity? We all want to be discovered, pursued, loved deeply, and restored to our best self, and fairy tales give us this. They provide a story where our deepest desires and wishes come true: good wins over evil, true love is found, and goodness lasts forever.

In addition, fairy tales and stories teach us valuable lessons and inspire us in many ways. Within fairy tales, we see age-old themes of good and evil, love and sacrifice, friendship and loyalty, ramifications for evil deeds, rewards for our choices, and much more.

The One Kingdom Adventure

As counselors, we have been helping couples for over twenty years experience healthier, happier marriages. We are always on the lookout for good analogies to better illustrate the abstract and complex concepts inherent in relationships. Analogies and imagery that stir the hearts of men and women and inspire us to be better people, parents, and partners. We found what we were looking for in the great stories of old past down throughout the generations in every culture around the world: fairy tales. Some details may vary for each time and era, but fairy tales stir within each of us the longing we are destined for—a great story with a special someone, one that ends happily forever.

We reasoned, if fairy tales resonate with our hearts as well as teach us important values throughout the centuries and cultures, why can't they be a powerful tool to teach us about marriages today?

With that in mind, we have written our own One Kingdom fairy tale that outlines the journey and the ebb and flow we have seen repeated in countless marriages.

We call our approach to helping couples the One Kingdom adventure; it is the culmination of our studies and experiences and reveals a groundbreaking approach to the marital model. The One Kingdom approach combines faith concepts, the latest research, and cultural evidence.

In this book, we want to teach you the basic concepts of One Kingdom.

Too many couples fall into the trap of believing that "happily ever after" begins the moment we say "I do." The truth we've noticed is that the fairy-tale journey of most successful couples goes through seven stages, or destinations.

Here's a brief description of the seven destinations you will likely discover along your fairy-tale journey:

- **Hills of Pursuit**

  Ah, to be young and in love! This is everyone's favorite part of the love cycle, where we woo and pursue our partner. You're on your best behavior, sparks are flying, and life is one exciting adventure after another.

- **Purple Meadows**

  The chase is over and your love is official. Your lover can do no wrong, and you're both selflessly serving each other and appreciating your differences. You enjoy one another, and purple abounds (when the pink and blue kingdoms come together)! If only you could stay here forever . . .

- **Dark Forest**

  The perfect romance is blindsided by conflict and sudden darkness. Every relationship encounters it, and it leaves you wounded, bitter, and vulnerable. It's vital that you learn how to fight together for your love's survival.

- **Queen School**

  Knowledge is power, and the truth will set you free. Here, men learn what really inspires and invigorates women. The secret to making good investments is revealed, and kings discover what it means to truly know their queen.

- **King School**

  What really drives and awakens men? Here, women learn about the power of words to capture the heart and soul of their king. Armed with these insights, queens discover what it means to become an honoring partner.

- **Garden of Love**

  At last, your love takes flight in ways you could never have imagined. True love, built with mutual trust, devotion, and transparency, transforms your relationship. It's the perfect garden—no secrets.

- **Royal Castle**

  You rule your kingdom as one—a united king and queen. The Royal Castle is a place of peace and mutuality where true love endures for a lifetime. You treasure and inspire your partner, build a legacy, and live happily ever after.

In the following chapters, we're going to teach you key principles inherent in each of the seven destinations. We're also going to show you the heart longing experienced at each destination—and give you the key to meeting the longing of your spouse at every stage of your journey.

In the process, you will

- Discover that fairy-tale love—the kind of love we all crave but which is often dismissed as immature, unrealistic, and imaginary—is indeed within your grasp.
- Realize that men want a storybook love as much as women.
- Learn that storybook romance is a deep yearning of the heart, one that God planted in each of us.
- Rediscover your passion for your partner and learn to love each other in a totally new way.
- Become wise to the evidence of epic love stories all around us—and be inspired to begin writing and living your own!

Participate Online to Get the Most from This Adventure

To support you on this journey, we have also created an online video curriculum that will take you deeper into the concepts discussed in this book as well as help you apply them to your relationship.

Here's how the online video series works:

- Each lesson begins with a video of the One Kingdom fairy tale that will provide you with clues and a brief introduction of what the lesson will entail.

- The intro video is followed by about 25–35 minutes of teaching by us (Jake and Jenn).
- In each lesson we discuss one of the seven destinations, which parallel the stages a relationship goes through as outlined earlier. At each destination we identify a specific heart longing and give you a key designed to meet that longing in your spouse—and help your spouse meet that longing in you.
- Each lesson ends with workbook and reflection time that takes about 10–15 minutes to complete. After individually completing the workbook, you and your spouse will be encouraged to share your thoughts and insights with each other.
- Each session takes approximately 45 minutes to an hour to complete.

The book you hold in your hands and the video series complement each other, and we encourage you to use both as you explore new vistas in your relationship.

Enroll in the video experience at www.onekingdom.us, and use promo code "1Kbook" for 20 percent off!

We look forward to sharing this journey with you and would love to hear your story of how One Kingdom inspired you to live *your* fairy tale. When you visit www.onekingdom.us, you'll find a contact page where you can share your thoughts with us, inquire about speaking engagements and events, or learn more about private counseling.

Who is this book for? It is for anyone longing for a rich story and a partner to create it with. Although our studies, experience, and research are primarily in the area of cisgender men and women and heterosexual couples, we believe this book and these concepts can be applied by any couple longing for a great adventure with longevity and fulfillment. We also do not presume to understand or speak to the complicated issues that same-gender or other couples face. Therefore, we humbly stay in our field of expertise without the intent of excluding or dismissing same-sex couples and more.

May you feel some camaraderie in knowing we are writing our fairy tale right along with you.

Here's to your "happily ever after"!

—Drs. Jake and Jenn

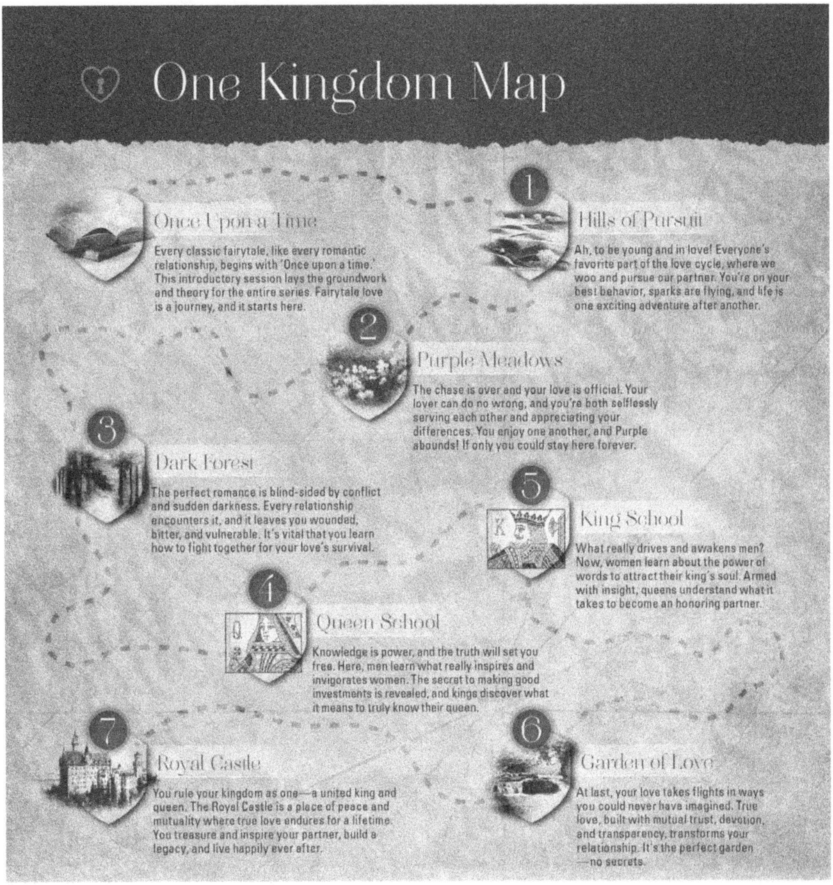
One Kingdom Map
Once Upon a Time
Every classic fairytale, like every romantic relationship, begins with 'Once upon a time.' This introductory session lays the groundwork and theory for the entire series. Fairytale love is a journey, and it starts here.
1
Hills of Pursuit
Ah, to be young and in love! Everyone's favorite part of the love cycle, where we woo and pursue our partner. You're on your best behavior, sparks are flying, and life is one exciting adventure after another.
2
Purple Meadows
The chase is over and your love is official. Your lover can do no wrong, and you're both selflessly serving each other and appreciating your differences. You enjoy one another, and Purple abounds! If only you could stay here forever.
3
Dark Forest
The perfect romance is blind-sided by conflict and sudden darkness. Every relationship encounters it, and it leaves you wounded, bitter, and vulnerable. It's vital that you learn how to fight together for your love's survival.
5
King School
What really drives and awakens men? Now, women learn about the power of words to attract their king's soul. Armed with insight, queens understand what it takes to become an honoring partner.
4
Queen School
Knowledge is power, and the truth will set you free. Here, men learn what really inspires and invigorates women. The secret to making good investments is revealed, and kings discover what it means to truly know their queen.
7
Royal Castle
You rule your kingdom as one—a united king and queen. The Royal Castle is a place of peace and mutuality where true love endures for a lifetime. You treasure and inspire your partner, build a legacy, and live happily ever after.
6
Garden of Love
At last, your love takes flights in ways you could never have imagined. True love, built with mutual trust, devotion, and transparency, transforms your relationship. It's the perfect garden —no secrets.

One Kingdom

1

THE FAIRY-TALE RECIPE

Once upon a time, in a faraway land, there lived a prince and princess. The prince, from his blue kingdom, was strong and valiant; he lived for adventure and conquest, a hero who battled dragons and defended castles. The princess, from her pink kingdom, was radiant and virtuous; she longed for destiny and possibility, a dreamer who spread hope wherever she went. As chance would have it, the prince and princess crossed paths, and at once they were taken with one another. It was as if destiny had joined the two, and a vision of one kingdom grew within them.

When I (Jenn) was a child, my dad told us the best fairy tales. When he would come in to tuck my sister and me into bed, we'd beg him to tell us a story. I can still remember being tucked in under my rose quilted bedspread, with pink sponge curlers in my hair, waiting with wide-eyed anticipation for my dad as he said the magical words "Once upon a time . . ."

As soon as he said those words, I was transported to another time and place where anything could happen, adventure beckoned, and heroes and villains greeted me. I still feel a shiver up my spine when I hear a fairy tale introduced with those familiar words.

When you hear the words "Once upon a time," you just know a great story is about to unfold.

My husband, Jake, and I studied what makes the best fairy tales—the ones that resonate deep in our hearts—and determined that there are three parts to the kind of "happily ever after" story we all long to experience.

And it's no wonder that part 1 of what we call the Fairy-Tale Recipe begins with the very words that evoked awe in our hearts as children from almost the first time we heard them.

Fairy-Tale Recipe Part 1.
The Beginning: "Once upon a time . . ."

The Fairy-Tale Recipe begins, as do all great fairy tales, with four little words: Once upon a time.

At the beginning of the story, you enter in a time and place very different from your own, and you meet the main characters.

Right away in the story, you discover that the main characters are each suffering from a deep, unmet desire. Perhaps they desire to win the heart of someone they love, to conquer evil, to defend the wronged, or to discover a treasure.

Whatever the desire, you also discover that the story's main characters are willing to make great sacrifices in order to satisfy their desires.

The adventure begins to unfold around that unmet desire:

> Cinderella is given a chance to go to a ball and find the prince.
>
> Ariel is willing to give up her mermaid tail and voice in exchange for legs.
>
> The beast is running out of time to receive love's true kiss from Belle.

Fairy-Tale Recipe Part 2.
The Conflict: "Will the longing get met?"

Now, this is where the story starts getting *really* good.

In every fairy tale, there is a villain determined to stop the main characters from ever experiencing that "happily ever after."

Cinderella's nemesis is her own evil stepmother. Snow White's, the witch. Belle and the beast have to overcome a magical curse placed by a witch.

These villains made us shiver when we were kids—and perhaps they still do! These enemies of goodness have no integrity, mercy, or compassion, and will stop at nothing to hinder our heroes from reaching happiness. And if our heroes possess anything of value, they will be relentlessly pursued by the greedy villain trying to claim it for their own.

But wait! In all good fairy tales, eventually we meet the hero helper. This supernatural influence might appear as magic, as the

White Witch, as a fairy godmother, as wisps, or as a genie. But what they all have in common is that these supernatural beings can make the impossible possible.

They help the hero fulfill his or her longing—but a sacrifice is always required. He or she must give up something of great value. Cinderella has only a certain amount of time to go to the ball and then has to return to her sisters in rags. Ariel has to leave her life under the sea and give up her precious voice if she wants to be with the prince of her dreams.

And in most fairy tales, with that sacrifice and a little magic, wonderful things eventually happen.

Not right away, of course.

But eventually.

Which leads us to part 3 of our Fairy-Tale Recipe . . .

Fairy-Tale Recipe Part 3.
The Ending/Resolution: "And they lived happily ever after . . ."

Notice the word *they*.

This is a key to the happy ending of the story. After all, what kind of a story would it be if it ended this way: "After Prince Charming married the princess, he decided he liked his bachelor life better, so he left her in the castle to go explore his own life without her"?

Or what if a fairy tale ended like this: "The prince lived on happily, ignoring the fact that the princess hated their life together and often wished she had left him in the form of a toad."

How anti-climactic, depressing, and even tragic these endings would be!

There are no happy hermits. For our story to end happily, both partners must share in that happiness.

Now notice the words that come after *they*: "They *lived happily* . . ."

That means our prince and princess don't just survive—they *thrive*. Again, the beauty of a great fairy tale is how the relationship doesn't merely *survive* the horrors of a dark forest, a wicked witch, or a poisonous substance, but it goes on to *thrive*. When you see the truly victorious couple sharing true love's kiss at the altar during a majestic wedding, you walk away feeling complete, as if that's exactly how it's supposed to end.

After all, how can you beat the appeal of a couple living happily in a blissful union, better and stronger from the victorious adventure they shared together?

And now let's look at the rest of the phrase: "They lived happily *ever after*!"

The truth is that every one of us harbors the desire for something to last forever. Indeed, God has placed eternity in the hearts of humans—a longing for eternal love and life—that makes us long for that ultimate happy ending. We want to experience life where death is cheated, love is unfailing, good triumphs over evil, and the supernatural delivers the ultimate ending to our story.

Does the Fairy-Tale Recipe resonate with you?

Like marriage, fairy tales reflect the deepest longings of men and women. And since fairy tales promise us that our longings *can* be met, shouldn't marriage promise the same?

As couples, we long for a great adventure. After all, every great fairy tale includes an adventure or a quest. In fairy tales, often that unattainable desire is met (against all odds!) in a triumphant and magical way. The story ends with resolution and success—and often true love!

Why shouldn't our marriage adventures end the same way?

When life doesn't feel like a fairy tale

Now, I suspect you may be thinking, "Yes, that's what I've always longed for, but unfortunately I've learned that happy endings are make-believe and that real life never turns out that way."

Are you sure? Perhaps this has been your reality so far, but just because you have experienced pain doesn't mean that joy isn't around the corner. In fact, happiness can never be felt or expressed without knowing the opposite of happiness, which is hurt or pain.

Some people, after experiencing disappointment, shut down emotionally to keep from experiencing more pain—but in the process they shut out hope, happiness, and joy. If you divorce yourself from pain or sadness, then you have also divorced yourself from pleasure and joy, and life becomes a dull, bland existence.

I get it. When our "in love" feelings don't last forever, our endings don't happen happily, and life seems to be full of dead-end connections, it's disappointing. Devastating even.

Men and women can stop dreaming, seeking, and believing that they are designed to have their own fairy tale. They forget that every great fairy tale has its share of dark forests and evil villains—and they get lost in their own dark forest of despair and hopelessness.

Disillusioned couples stop longing or seeking to meet the longings of their partner. They become consumed with despair, disappointment, and hopelessness as they dismiss the very stories that have survived for centuries.

They stop their quest to embrace "happily ever after" with the partner they once loved deeply—and they start dreaming about a new "happily ever after" apart from their partner. Instead of going on a quest to create a new adventure with their partner, or working together to find a way out of the dark forest, they quit, become bitter, and throw away the map in discouragement.

When couples reach this place, they often think they have come to the end of their story.

But the truth is, they are in the *middle* of their story!

They are in the part where it looks like the evil stepmother, witch, or dark spell is winning.

But this doesn't mean that "happily ever after" is make-believe.

It just means there is more to be written.

So what goes wrong?

Why do couples get stuck in the middle of their stories? Why are they tempted to close the book before the happy ending can be embraced?

We work with a lot of couples, and one of the first questions we always ask is, "When was the last time you dated each other?"

Too many times we get a blank stare, as they finally come up with, "I can't remember."

This is the key to their success and failure. We need to remember, we are still writing our fairy tale for our relationship, and we are the authors of our own relationship story.

As therapists, we are burdened by the reoccurring and familiar issues that threaten couples today.

Below are the five biggest challenges we see couples facing today.

Challenge #1: Fear

We believe the breakdown in marriage begins with fear.

Out of fear of being run over, hurt, or dismissed, we cling to our own kingdoms of pink and blue and use our energy to develop our defenses instead of creating a mutually satisfying One Kingdom.

Couples stop loving and believing in each other and start fearing and distrusting each other, and the bond grows weak between them. The passion leaves and the partners begin living parallel lives with no interactive, passionate exchanges between them.

Challenge #2: Lack of collaboration

When fear goes unaddressed, connecting behavior—the kind that builds a strong, secure, and loving bond—is often replaced by controlling behavior. One person (or both!) can begin to dominate the relationship, exhibiting low empathy for the feelings and needs of his or her partner and a low value for developing a collaborative partnership.

The truth is that we work with many couples who face this challenge (and we would be lying if we told you we have never wrestled with it ourselves!).

It takes concerted effort to choose love and mutuality, rejecting selfish fear and independence focused on your own needs over those of your partner.

When couples are unable or unwilling to collaborate, they can experience conflict and unfair fighting, which destroys the fibers of their relationship.

Challenge #3: Gender conflict, or not appreciating each other's differences

Too many couples tragically misunderstand each other and build their relationship on misguided beliefs of one another.

When this happens, we can take offense at our partner due to our lack of understanding of the uniqueness of men and women, and spend our energy trying to change and correct each other versus learning to accept and appreciate each other.

Challenge #4: Impatience

We believe this is a major contributor to the rising divorce rate. Couples lose hope too soon and quit on the marriage. They naively believe in "love at first sight" and the magical thinking around "instant soul mates." But they give up too early, before real work can make a difference and turn their situations around.

The truth is that love takes time to develop—experts say it takes as long as twenty years to develop a soul-mate status in a relationship.

This lack of relationship knowledge leads to unrealistic expectations and failed relationships, which leads to a lack of hope for young couples to pursue marriage or a committed relationship, as the number of divorces rises.

Challenge #5: Misunderstood concept of oneness

Developing oneness in your relationship is a journey, and it doesn't happen just because you get married.

When we got married, Jenn's mother pulled us aside and gave us these adamant instructions: "When you light the unity candle, don't blow out your individual candles. Keep them lit!"

We did as she instructed—and as a result heard from many people that we had made a mistake with our unity candle. Still, we didn't regret it—and also didn't realize how symbolic that act would become for us.

To have a strong oneness in the relationship, you need to have a strong "me." The more individuated you are from your family of origin, the easier it is to differentiate from your partner in a relationship.

Couples want oneness and "happily ever after," but they don't know how to get there. The good news is that now, more than ever, we are learning and developing more realistic expectations of relationships. Therapy has become a formalized profession in helping people create stability individually and in relationships. The relationship coaching profession is also on the rise to assist couples in moving through their issues, and experts are discovering what makes people bond chemically and emotionally.

As a society, we are beginning to understand and redefine the success of a relationship—and what it takes to create that kind of bond.

This knowledge and these tools are available for us to apply to our own marriages—it just takes some awareness, practice, hope, and help.

Challenge #6: Unrealistic expectations

Early in my marriage to Jake, we went go-carting with another couple and received very poor service from the employees. I (Jenn) was frustrated and angry about our experience and wanted compensation for our troubles. As I heard Jake talk to the manager, I expected him to be more assertive in getting a refund for the poor service.

When I expressed frustration to my friend who was with us, he simply said, "That's not Jake."

That was a formative moment for reshaping my image of Jake and having realistic expectations of who he was—rather than who I wanted him to be.

Unrealistic expectations can also stem from wanting a partner to be "all things all the time." To expect a partner to meet *all* our needs creates too much pressure for the relationship to thrive under. We need same-gender friendships to offer us what our partner cannot.

When marriage partners have no friends or activities outside of each other, the dependency can become stifling. We need others to help shape and refine us—and to meet some of our needs too.

We all want the same things.

As therapists, we realized we needed to offer a new solution to the failing marriages often stuck in perpetual conflict and tension.

After listening for over fifteen years to couples in therapy, we noticed a pattern. Everyone had longings they were trying to meet, regardless of their gender. These were often the underlying messages struggling to come forward in the everyday conflicts that seemed to plague couples perpetually.

Everyone wants to be

- Chosen
- Appreciated
- Protected
- Honored
- Known
- Loved
- Inspired

Time and time again, when these longings go unmet, we see individuals fighting to matter, to be appreciated, loved, and protected—sometimes without ever speaking up and voicing their unmet needs to their partners!

Sometimes that struggle for significance, appreciation, love, and protection can damage the relationship as hurting people turn to bullying, manipulation, and fighting to get their needs met.

And let's be honest—gender differences don't help matters either. The gender differences in processing styles, self-expression, and even biology complicate our communications with each other from the very beginning.

Finally, it's tempting to buy into the idea that "happily ever after" has to look a certain way and there's only one path to get there. As a society, we don't encourage creative marriage models for relationships—yet sometimes that's exactly what must happen in order to live our storybook dreams.

But despite the challenges, the deep longings are very real—and they are universal.

We are all longing for the same things.

It's easy to dismiss fairy tales as "child's play" and to come to the sad conclusion that "happily ever after" is only for storybooks and not for real relationships.

But the good news is that "happily ever after" *is* possible. Even better, it is God's design for our marriages.

The greatest story ever told

The greatest storybook of all, the Bible, starts with the words "In the beginning . . ."

In other words, the Bible begins with its own version of "Once upon a time . . ."

We're not saying the Bible is make-believe. Quite the opposite. And it is our inspiration for working with couples.

Here is what our Creator said about couples during creation:

> Then God said, "Let us make mankind in our image, in our likeness, so that they may rule over the fish in the sea and the birds in the sky, over the livestock and all the wild animals, and over all the creatures that move along the ground." (Genesis 1:26)

> God blessed them and said to them, "Be fruitful and increase in number; fill the earth and subdue it. Rule over the fish in the sea and the birds in the sky and over every living creature that moves on the ground." (Genesis 1:28)

> God saw all that he had made, and it was very good. (Genesis 1:31)

> That is why a man leaves his father and mother and is united to his wife, and they become one flesh. Adam and his wife were both naked, and they felt no shame. (Gen 2:24–25)

These verses paint a clear picture of four powerful truths about marriage:

1. God made the earth for man and woman to rule together, in mutuality and harmony.

2. He loved what he created!
3. Leaving the old and embracing the new with your partner as you become one is a process that takes time and understanding.
4. This is the ultimate "happily ever after": to live in a relationship void of shame and full of transparency while honoring one another. The opposite of shame is grace or honor. So because they felt no shame, Adam and Eve accepted and honored each other while they lived naked and open with each other.

If these verses portray the original and ultimate model for couples, one question remains: How do we get there?

And we've got an answer for you.

Your One Kingdom Fairy Tale

We see marriage as a fairy tale, waiting to be written and told. Danger, conflict, pain, death may be part of your story—in fact, it's pretty much guaranteed—but these plot twists don't have to rob you of your happy ending or fulfilling moments.

How we choose to respond to the dark forest that often envelops us is what makes our fairy-tale story. After all, a story without *any* evil, villains, or dark forest would not make for an exciting fairy tale. Living a perfect life without any highs and lows is not the spirit of fairy tales.

What's at the heart of the very best stories? Obstacles, hardships, and challenges. Fighting for your very life and the love you are seeking, all the while conquering death, fears, and menacing villains in hope for a better existence with someone by your side.

And the destination? A place where the couple has the power to rule their One Kingdom with equity, love, and hope. Where the light is stronger than the darkness, love conquers all, and divine help is given for the couple to rule their kingdom successfully.

Allow us to introduce . . . One Kingdom.

One Kingdom is about eliminating the power struggle created when women and men seek to protect their individual domains—which we call the pink and blue kingdoms—at the expense of what God designed us to create—and enjoy—together.

One Kingdom is about identifying universal longings, then discovering the keys to meet those longings so you can go on to discover your own "happily ever after."

One Kingdom is a place where individual kingdoms are not eliminated but are remade into something entirely new and game-changing: a united kingdom of purple.

REFLECTION

What's your definition of fairy-tale love?

What's your favorite fairy tale and character, and why?

What do you believe marriages are lacking the most?

List some things you hope to learn from this book.

2

JAKE AND JENN'S ONE KINGDOM FAIRY TALE

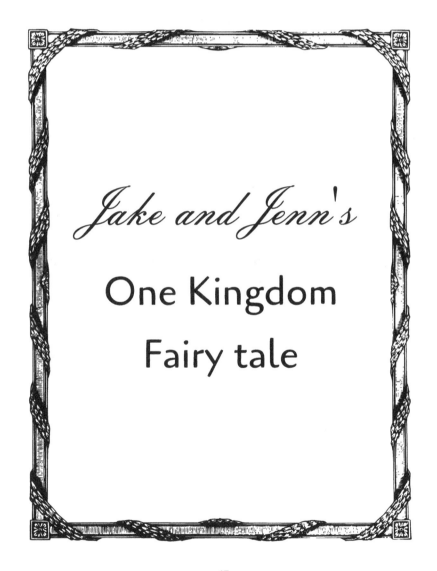

Jake and Jenn's

One Kingdom Fairy tale

Before we get started navigating the first of the seven destinations, we want to show you what these destinations have looked like in our own kingdom story. After all, in addition to counseling hundreds of couples, we are living our own fairy-tale story and have experienced the beauty and challenges of these destinations in our own lives.

Let's start at the beginning.

Once upon a time, there was a prince named Jake and a princess named Jenn . . .

Enjoying the Hills of Pursuit

Our chapter in the Hills of Pursuit began when we met at Azusa Pacific University. Although we met our freshman year, we didn't start dating until the end of our senior year.

As college sweethearts, we pursued each other while pursuing our education and individual interests. When we had the opportunity to work together with the same youth group, we realized not only were we crazy about each other, but our gifts and callings complemented each other and we were well suited as partners.

Beginning our trek through the Purple Meadows

We were married in 1993, marking the end of our romp through the Hills of Pursuit.

As a committed couple, we ventured into the Purple Meadows, where we began to create a life together. We knew how important it was to build a united kingdom that honored both of us. As a symbol of that honor and respect, we took each other's last names in a hyphenated form to symbolize equity and to build our One Kingdom.

We ministered at a church together, continuing our work with youth while Jenn also worked as a middle school teacher. Our lives and dreams continued to meld with the birth of two children (a boy and a girl) and the launch of our therapy practice.

A sacred season in the Dark Forest

The best stories include their share of obstacles, dark turns, and plot twists—and ours is no exception.

Several years into our marriage, we found ourselves taking an unplanned detour through the Dark Forest.

Our kids were toddlers, and Jake was working long hours in church ministry as a pastor. Jenn decided to be a stay-at-home mom after completing her master's in social work, because that's what she thought she had to do.

Yet Jenn missed her work with youth and ministry to couples and families, and found herself sliding into a constant state of restlessness and depression. Plus, with Jake working his long hours, she often felt alone and isolated.

Jake was on autopilot in a job that demanded more than he was able to provide, and he missed his kids and family.

In the Dark Forest the vision of why we came together began to dim. Our dream of working together to raise a family while empowering others felt out of reach. We felt stuck and were in perpetual conflict about time, family, and extended family.

In the process, deep longings and dreams were going unmet in each of us—and we felt powerless to change or recapture our vision for our future. We were lost and wandering. And the more we listened to well-meaning advice from society and others on how to live our lives, the more lost we became.

Eventually we decided to turn a deaf ear to society's persistent chatter about who we were supposed to be as a couple and individuals.

We reminded each other of who we were, what each of us wanted out of life, and what we wanted our future to look like. Then, and only then, could we begin to navigate our way out of the Dark Forest. We set out on a path we'd been told would lead nowhere—which turned into the very thing we needed not just to survive but to thrive.

We'll be honest with you: our chapter in the Dark Forest was scary. We soon realized, however, that it also was a sacred time in our journey together.

With a few hundred dollars to our name, a new mortgage, two toddlers, and a ton of disappointments and hurts, we left the security of our jobs and opened a private counseling practice.

We'd been told we were too young to succeed and that we didn't have enough life experience or financial security. But we'd seen the light through the trees at the end of the forest, and we were determined to keep going.

It wasn't easy.

As she built her practice, Jenn was still reeling from the births of our two children and taking care of two toddlers.

As he built his practice, Jake left a desk job and worked construction part-time.

Although it was a struggle, we were finding our way out of the Dark Forest in which we'd felt stuck and imprisoned, and our struggles seemed light in comparison. We pursued our vision of coparenting while both us provided for our family, which later became identified as a Peer Marriage model.

Even though the Dark Forest was behind us, we still had some important lessons to learn.

Learning life-changing lessons in King and Queen School

Jake was coming to realize that some of the ways he was perceiving and treating Jenn were having disastrous results.

He realized he kept expecting her to think and react to life like he did, and he had a hard time appreciating her differences. Jake often struggled with caring or paying attention to who Jenn was and would "forget" to respect her differences. Covert bullying and manipulative behavior had become a way for him to get his longings met, and boundaries were not acknowledged or respected.

In a powerful life-altering moment, Jake made a commitment to improve his knowledge of his queen. He realized his energies needed to go into accepting Jenn and paying attention to who she was, rather than simply tolerating her. He also needed to learn how to accept the ways Jenn was different from him and how to appreciate her qualities so he could better complement her.

And so began what we like to call his enrollment in Queen School.

Soon he realized the results he received were much more satisfying when he used his energy to validate her and empower her to meet her longings and achieve her callings.

Even today, anytime his interactions with Jenn feel uncertain or confusing, he takes a quick trip to Queen School by asking her two very important questions:

1. "What are you feeling?"
2. "What do you need?"

Then he sets out to help her in the best way possible without disrespecting who he is.

(A note from Jenn: As I write this, Jake is drilling a hole in my bathroom wall to provide a new outlet for my curling iron. I love this man!)

Jenn had her own lessons to learn.

Her enrollment in King School began as she realized she was trying to change Jake and teach him how to be a more "evolved" man instead of simply expressing her own needs, feelings, and boundaries to him. She had spent lots of years in this futile effort, which caused her to lose sight not only of him but of herself. Overt bullying and mean words had become a way for her to get her longings met and to strive to be seen by or matter with Jake. She found herself speaking and behaving in ways that were against her values, and realized she was not using her energies to understand and accept who Jake was or what he felt and needed.

Realizing she needed to learn how to accept the ways Jake was different from her, and how to appreciate his qualities so she could better complement him, Jenn began being a better student of Jake. This, in turn, made her a better student and ambassador of herself as she spent valuable energy better representing who she was to him as well as accepting who he was to her.

Even today, anytime Jenn feels resentful, angry, or confused, she takes a quick jaunt back to King School by asking Jake two powerful questions:

1. "What are you feeling?"
2. "What do you need?"

Suspending any judgment, guilt, or shame at his answers, she sets about helping him get his expressed needs met out of love for him and herself. She makes a conscious effort to stay out of the FOG—that is, the FOG of *f*ear, *o*bligation, and *g*uilt—as she helps him meet his needs.

Discovering the long-awaited Garden of Love

Today, we are definitely journeying into the Garden of Love. This is the stage we are entering into as true partners. Soul-mate status is where our relationship is headed, and we are excited about it. We have put in the time and earned our stripes!

Now we are ready to cash in on lots of hard work at establishing our One Kingdom together and to enjoy the fruits of our labor.

As we ask ourselves what our story looks like at this destination, here's what we're noticing:

- Humor, acceptance, and real conversations are being had with more ease.
- Past hurts are dimming, and forgiveness is a daily gift.
- We feel real joy.
- Conflict is more productive.
- Anytime we find ourselves looping back into the Dark Forest, we are able to exit with more speed and more reserves.
- We consciously choose a peaceful community together, full of love, grace, and adventure.

There is no such thing as a perfect marriage, but we are proud of the fairy tale we are writing together. We also love the shared faith we have in a God who has lovingly and tenderly carried us through some dark times. Finally, we are looking with anticipation toward the future, with less struggle in our marriage and more focus on combining our resources to benefit our world.

But there's still more that we can do.

What's next?

Royal Castle, here we come!

In our opinion, this is what makes a great marriage: providing a home for each individual to live their greatness while drawing from the powerful collaborative fuel a secure partnership can offer. Which is why, as we are entering the empty-nest stage of life, we are looking forward to leaving a legacy and living together happily as best we can—this is our quest and the heart of our fairy tale.

We are starting to ask ourselves questions like these:

"What do we want to leave behind?"
"How do we want to be remembered?"
"How do we want our kids to remember us?"
"What do we want to create individually and together?"

Our unique perspectives on marriage and human behavior have been shaped by what we've discovered together, and our mutual private practices have given us rich insights that are inspiring and restoring marriages nationwide. Creating a loving, grace-filled. and mutual community together where we are both leaders and servants has created a powerful resource for us to live our best lives.

We have found great joy in not only meeting community needs through volunteer work but also introducing our kids to third world needs. Through the World Help organization, we have formed valuable relationships and friendships, and have thoroughly enjoyed providing clean water wells to communities desperately in need of clean water.

Our kids are a part of our legacy, and what we teach and expose them to has the potential to create exponential change in our world. Investing in them has been a privilege and an honor and a great use of our resources. We look forward to the legacy they will pass on to their kids, and it starts with us, as it started with our parents and grandparents.

So that's our fairy tale in a nutshell, and it is still being actively and courageously lived out.

Like you, we still have our Dark Forest moments, days, and weeks—and are committed to creating a different story and connection. More than ever, we know that our Dark Forest seasons produce sacred moments.

Perfection is never the goal.

Instead, the goal is living a story of which we can be proud—and a story that may be inspiring to others.

Now let's talk about *you* . . .

In the coming chapters, we're going to talk about *your* story and the role these seven destinations play in your fairy-tale love story.

And as we give you an overview of each destination, we will explore three main areas:

- **The Heart Longing** most deeply felt at each destination

- **The Crisis** that threatens your success
- **The Key** to meeting this heart longing in your spouse—and the key to your spouse meeting this heart longing in you—at this and every destination and stage of your journey

Because here's the thing.

The seven heart longings you're about to discover play important roles in their respective seven destinations. In fact, your ongoing skills at meeting these heart longings in your partner will forge a rock-solid foundation for the One Kingdom you are building together. This is an adventure you get to create as a couple, where you each get to be the hero and heroine of your story.

REFLECTION

Which parts of Jake and Jenn's story resonated the most with you and why?

Can you identify what part of the fairytale journey you and your partner may currently be experiencing?

When you hear about challenges other couples have faced, how does it make you feel? Discouraged? Hopeful? Explain.

What part of your fairytale journey did you love the most or are you looking forward to the most and why?

3

HILLS OF PURSUIT

Before long, the prince and princess were inseparable. The prince adorned his finest armor and made great displays of strength to gain her attention, for she had enchanted him. The prince wooed her with the utmost time and attention—fixing his eyes on her every movement and his ears on her every word. With great discipline he studied her, for this was the conquest of his life. Wherever the princess went, he followed, guarding her steps with zeal and pride. The heart of the princess leaped with excitement, and her affection for the prince ignited. He could do no wrong, and her respect and admiration for the prince was without measure. She fancied herself with the finest oils, perfumes, and jewels to captivate her prince. Together they danced and played, eager for any adventure as long as they were together. Soon they were married, and the wedding celebrations were enjoyed throughout the kingdom.

PART ONE:
NAVIGATING THE HILLS OF PURSUIT

Ah, to be young and in love! You remember what this was like, don't you? After all, what's not to love about the Hills of Pursuit?

This is everyone's favorite part of the love cycle, where we woo and pursue our partner. You're on your best behavior, sparks are flying, and life is one exciting adventure after another.

As we navigate the Hills of Pursuit, we're going to explore three aspects:

- **The Heart Longing** most deeply felt at this destination *("Choose me!")*
- **The Crisis** that threatens your success *(Not Being Chosen)*
- **The Key** to meeting this heart longing *(Create Adventure)*

Perhaps you are currently in the middle of this stage of your relationship. Maybe you're well into marriage and feel like these days are behind you.

Either way, keep reading! This chapter has something important for you.

While each destination has a primary heart longing, these longings don't disappear when we reach the next destination. These are longings that must continue to be met for you and your spouse throughout your entire marriage!

Now, let's dive in.

The Heart Longing: "Choose Me!"

Everyone wants to be pursued, wanted, and chosen above all others.

When I (Jenn) was in middle school, I was tiny, uncoordinated, and nonathletic. So when it came to choosing teams, it was to my chagrin when I was usually chosen last. My occasional saving grace—depending on the sport for which teams were being chosen—was the fact that I was a fast runner.

I can still feel the shame creeping up in my face at being overlooked time and time again, as the leader chose more coordinated and athletic team members.

To be overlooked, dismissed, neglected and ignored hurts to the core of any individual. Conversely, to be chosen first above all others speaks to our value as a human being.

Cinderella is the most told fairy tale worldwide and has been told in almost every culture for generations. Different renditions have surfaced, but the theme is the same, and we believe it's because in the tale she is desperately sought after and chosen by a great prince.

When Cinderella is transformed from her rags to a beautiful princess, it represents how she has always longed to be perceived, instead of how others have seen her.

When she is pursued by a powerful and influential prince, it strengthens her hope and belief that she may be more than her wicked stepmother and stepsisters have claimed her to be.

When the enchantment ends and the Cinderella gown returns to rags, the prince looks long and hard to find her. Even though he finds her back among the ashes, he has already seen her in her glory and sees her for who she really is.

He chooses her above all the women in the land.

We all want to be chosen, even when we're not so beautiful. We want people—and the more powerful, the better—to see potential in us and call that into fruition. And if you think this longing is just unique to women, think again.

We are all familiar with how the frog longs to be the chosen one, kissed and loved by the princess in his frog state, so he can return to his princely state.

Similarly, in the timeless tale of *Beauty and the Beast*, the beast longs to be loved by the beauty so he may also be redeemed and restored to his former life and image as a handsome and powerful prince.

We want not only to be chosen but to be chosen in our worst state.

Just as important, we want to *keep being chosen*—not chosen for a season and then cast aside.

This is a common fear plaguing many women and now a growing number of men.

I'm chosen now, but what about ten years from now?

Will I be traded in for someone younger, more beautiful, and more powerful?

Will he or she still love me when I am old, wrinkly, and gray?

This happens far too often, all around us, right?

Men and women have affairs and choose someone else right under the nose of their "cherished" prince or princess.

If you and your partner are trying courageously to recover from this kind of wounding, we encourage you to refocus on this basic heart longing and choose your partner with your words, actions, and thoughts. Leave no room for your partner to doubt that you are choosing them today and every day. We also would highly recommend marriage counseling to help you through the devastation of infidelity and the rebuilding process.

When I (Jake) was in eighth grade, I enjoyed attending the eighth grade dances, which involved a strategic selection process for choosing your dancing partner. The girls lined up against one wall of the gymnasium, and the boys lined up against the opposite wall.

If you wanted to dance with someone, you sent your best friend across the gym floor to ask your love interest if he or she would like to dance with you.

If your best friend came back with a good report (and rejection was no longer a possibility), you would take the risk of approaching your love interest to request a dance.

Dancing itself was a risky enough activity, so to endure rejection on top of the ask was more than an eighth grader's heart could bear.

I remember how good it felt to be chosen by a girl to dance, especially if that girl was cute and someone I already liked.

When choosing someone, you must risk rejection and disappointment. However, the sad alternative—the loneliness of living a life unchosen or not choosing someone yourself—outweighs the risk.

When someone takes a risk to choose us, it increases our sense of value and has a significant impact on our self-esteem. We feel important, valued, and cherished.

We often hear that men want to be chosen when it comes to sex, and women want to be chosen when it comes to emotional connection. Although both genders have a need for both, to choose our mate in ways that matter specifically to them validates their feelings of worth.

We want to add a related idea.

Our children want to feeling chosen by us too.

Just as it is important to choose each other, it is important for our children to know that we chose them too.

Our daughter was "planned," but our son came fourteen months later and was dubbed "the best surprise ever!"

Jenn was almost two months along before she discovered she was pregnant. We hoped for a boy but didn't dare box God in on that one. When Dawson was born, we became concerned he might feel unchosen since he had gone undetected for three months after conception.

So when he was two years old, I (Jenn) began telling him a story that went like this:

"Once upon a time, I prayed to God for a beautiful little boy and God lined up all the boys till they went around the world *two* times!"

At this point in the story, Dawson would gesture with me for emphasis by holding up two fingers and saying, "Twice!"

I would continue the story: "And I came to each face and held it carefully and lovingly in my hands, until I came to your face . . ."

At this point in the story, I would take Dawson's face in my hands.

"And I looked up to God pleading, 'Please, oh please, can I have this one for my son?' God looked reluctantly at me, then longingly look at the face of Dawson and said, "Well, I'm not so sure. You see, that's my special one. I need you to take extra good care of him because he's extra special to Me.' To which I would respond enthusiastically, 'Oh yes, oh yes, I will! I promise I will take extra special care of him.' Then God granted me my wish, and as he handed him over to me, you could see a tear trickle down His face. For although He loaned him to me, God would miss his company greatly and would look forward to having him back again one day."

After the story, Dawson and I would sigh contentedly, feeling privileged to have each other's company. As he drifted off to sleep, I hoped he knew he had a mom who chose him above all others.

The Crisis: Not Being Chosen

When our longing to be chosen is not met, a crisis happens.

We feel rejected, which is one of our greatest fears as humans.

We become angry, hurt, and resentful. Jealousy often ensues as we watch "our" person pursue someone or something else.

And it doesn't even have to be another person! Indeed, the greatest common tragedy we see in marriages is how partners stop choosing each other, and work, family, religion, kids, and even pets become chosen over the partner.

Not feeling chosen affects our self-esteem and confidence and hurts our self-image. We feel as if we are not worthy of someone taking a risk to pursue us and invite us to something exciting.

We struggle to feel adequate or significant and behave in a guarded manner to protect ourselves from the searing pain of not being chosen . . . again.

Imagine being an individual who time after time gets overlooked, dismissed, discounted, and invalidated. It becomes more pain than a person can bear, and if he or she is fragile or a child, the pain of death seems less terrifying.

School shootings are often fueled by the fact that a teen has been bullied, rejected, or simply unseen by his teachers and peers. Almost exclusively, school shootings are committed by boys, because injuring others is how boys most commonly express their pain.

At the same time, it's not uncommon for girls to express pain through self-harm such as eating disorders, cutting, or other forms of self-harm. It is estimated that over ten million girls and women in the United States are dealing with an eating disorder, and it is the mental illness with the highest mortality rate.[1] Cutting is also on the rise and is expected to meet or exceed the numbers and stats of eating disorders soon.

In working with these women and girls, we often discover they have been subjected to experiences or messages that have left them feeling unchosen, convinced they are not beautiful or smart or powerful enough to be chosen. Struggling with societal messages about beauty, these women have often been told their bodies fall painfully short of the mark, their pain is invalid or unnecessary, and/or their bodies have value only when used for the pleasure of someone else. They are often neglected by their fathers, which feeds the unworthiness they wrestle with daily.

We want to matter, to be chosen by another, despite our looks, ability, or position in life.

In one couple's session, the wife was complaining angrily and critically that her spouse always put his kids before her. She expressed great anger and hurt with him, explaining that he'd been doing this for years.

I (Jenn) quietly said, "You want to be chosen."

She gave a huge sigh and an enthusiastic "Yes!" Then she turned to her husband and said with tears streaming down her face, "I want to be chosen!"

Mother Teresa put it best: "We have drugs for people with diseases like leprosy. But these drugs do not treat the main problem: the disease of being unwanted. That's what my sisters hope to provide. The sick and poor suffer even more from rejection than material want. Loneliness and the feeling of being unwanted is the most terrible poverty."

Regardless of gender, ethnicity, or age, we all want to be chosen for something special by someone special. It is our heart's cry to be chosen above everyone else to have an exciting life adventure with someone, to share the hope of a better life, to experience love, humor, and faithful attention.

In our best or worse states, in sickness and in health, till death do us part, we want to be the chosen object of someone's affection.

In the Hills of Pursuit, we are chosen not just for a day. Our dream is that we are chosen for a *lifetime*, receiving the exciting gift of experiencing life together.

The Key: Create Adventure

The thrill of being chosen may be of utmost importance during our romps through the Hills of Pursuit—but it never ceases to matter. No matter where you are in your relationship journey, your One Kingdom depends on choosing each other to share in the grand adventure of life day after day, decade after decade.

How do you make sure you and your partner continue to choose each other over all else?

The key to meeting this heart longing in your partner—and having your heart longing met as well—may be simpler than you think.

The key is to replicate the context in which you first pursued each other and fell in love.

The key is . . . adventure!

After all, during the Hills of Pursuit, you choose each other above all others for adventures together. It wasn't hard to do. After all, something as simple as a walk in the moonlight probably felt like an unexplored world of epic possibility! And the natural result of these shared adventures is romance.

Ironically, the word *romance* in its very definition refers to adventure. Romance actually means "adventure" in Latin: "a mysterious or fascinating quality or appeal, as of something adventurous, heroic, or strangely beautiful."

We all want to be chosen for romance and adventure or to choose someone with whom to experience romance and adventure. Any of us can have an adventure by ourselves—but with a special person of our choosing, it becomes that much more rewarding and exciting.

Author Michael Ventura says it best: "Marriage is a journey toward an unknown destination—the discovery that people must share is not only what they don't know about each other, but what they don't know about themselves."

PART TWO:
YOUR QUEST IN THE HILLS OF PURSUIT

It's possible that the Hills of Pursuit are behind you. You may already be a couple with someone and simply looking for ways to enrich your relationship.

One way to do this is by revisiting and even recreating the excitement of the first destination you visited on your journey to becoming a couple: Hills of Pursuit.

To do this, remember the strong link between creating adventure and romance. In other words, as you are intentional about creating new adventures to enjoy as a couple, the romance will follow!

Here are three ways to create more romance and adventure in your relationship:

1. Create adventure by having a shared quest.

Creating adventure is best done together. After all, no one wants to be dragged along on someone else's adventure or to be a sidekick on the adventure. There needs to be mutuality in our adventures.

Sometimes we *think* the other person wants what we want. But when we don't take the time to check in with our partner, we can make assumptions and fail to communicate expectations, and our adventures can have disastrous results.

As you plan an adventure for you and your spouse—or plan one together—ask questions like these:

- "How much blue or pink is in this adventure?"
- "Do our adventures lean heavily toward one kingdom or another—blue or pink—instead of the mutuality of purple?"
- "Am I being considerate in our adventures together?"
- "How can I choose purple for this and future adventures?"

Two examples of what *not* to do come to mind.

In college, I (Jenn) was invited on a date by a man we'll call "Mark."

Mark invited me on a bike ride. And if that sounds romantic, let me explain a little more. This turned out to be no ordinary bike ride. We crossed ravines and streams, climbed mountains, and carried the bikes through rough terrain.

This was the first and last date I went on with Mark.

Because our harrowing adventure sounded fun to Mark, he assumed it would be fun for me. He assumed wrong. Although I completed the date (my pride wouldn't let me quit or admit defeat), Mark lost out on future adventures with me because he didn't take into consideration our mutual interests.

One birthday, I (Jake) decided to surprise Jenn with a trip to Las Vegas to enjoy a Celine Dion concert. Although we were both looking forward to the excursion, I made the mistake of not checking in with Jenn as to what other activities on our trip would be enjoyable for both of us.

Being an architecture enthusiast, I made it my main mission to see every unique hotel on the Vegas strip in one afternoon, by foot.

Jenn dutifully accompanied me on this quest, until she realized how many there were and that my intent was to trudge on undaunted by the heat or expanse of our quest.

After about the eighth hotel, Jenn sat down under a shade tree and promptly announced she was done visiting all the hotels and would appreciate me remembering this was *her* birthday trip.

At that point I quickly and wisely accompanied her on a shopping excursion of her choosing.

There's something else to consider as you plan adventures together. Not every activity needs to be "purple." Sometimes it's okay to pursue an adventure that is more blue than pink as long as the next adventure is more pink than blue (or vice versa).

Here's an example.

One couple I (Jake) counseled was failing miserably in staying connected and creating oneness. In the course of their counseling sessions, it came out that the husband was unwilling to go to a fashion show with his wife, even though she had gone to his hockey games for years.

I explained to him that while you don't necessarily need to give up your personal interests, it's important to be considerate in meeting the desires of your partner, especially if your partner repeatedly comes into *your* kingdom to honor you. This requires trust and respect by both partners to achieve this unique and beautiful balance in creating purple adventures.

When this husband finally recognized the value of leaving his comfort zone to honor his wife and be considerate of her wants, connectedness and oneness were able to take root.

Relationships need ongoing adventures that invite each partner to leave behind what's familiar to them, branching out to create a royal, purple kingdom together.

2. Create adventure by taking risks together.

To create adventure, you sometimes need to take risks.

Taking risks can resurrect a dying relationship or take a healthy relationship from good to great. Whatever stage you're in, your relationship will benefit from taking Confident, Passionate Risks (CPR)—and sometimes every relationship needs a little CPR to come alive again.

Society counts on individuals willing to take risks. Throughout history we see how progress could never have been made if someone hadn't taken a risk. The Wright brothers would never have learned to fly if they had been unwilling to risk failure, public humiliation, and ultimately death. And without taking risks, Thomas Edison would never have invented the light bulb, and Bill Gates and Steve Jobs would never have turned their wildly imaginative ideas into the reality of home computers.

Just like society needs people, groups, and institutions to take risks so we can experience progress, we must be willing to take risks if we desire relational progress. We must be willing to risk our most valued possession—our heart—to see our dreams and desires turned into reality.

The confidence to risk everything and leave behind what is familiar and comfortable is needed to create adventure with your partner.

We certainly see risk taking in fairy tales, don't we? Before Ariel in *The Little Mermaid* found true love, she risked a lot: she left her entire world behind—including her tail!—and chose life in a "whole new world," complete with human legs! Ariel risked being shunned by her family and rejected by her prince—yet her deep desire to experience a different life and pursue true love created the confidence she needed to take life-altering risks.

In our counseling practice, we see marriages and relationships become stagnant when one or both partners become stagnant. It only takes one unimaginative person with no confidence to risk for the slow process of atrophy in a relationship to begin.

Besides, risks generate adrenaline. In fact, many men thrive on adrenaline. It is no coincidence that in relationships men are often the pursuers by initiating calls, dates, and proposals. Men thrive on adrenaline surges and often seek them out by participating in risky behavior.

And while women are often less inclined to take risks themselves, they can find risk-taking behavior in men exciting.

We remember one husband who bemoaned the loss of passion in his marriage. When we asked him how he and his wife met, he told us he was working construction on a rooftop when he spotted a beautiful girl riding a bike toward him. In a reckless move, he jumped off the rooftop to meet her—which thoroughly impressed her—and they spent the day together. She admired the reckless show of strength, confidence, and passion as he pursued her. Within two years they were married.

As he told us this story, he realized that over the years he had changed, becoming less confident and less willing to take risks.

It dawned on him that this had resulted in less passion and fewer adventures with his wife.

Passion can be derived from the "feel good hormone" Dopamine. When dopamine is increased through pleasurable activities such as sleep, food, exercise, sex, and more, this lays the fertile soil for passion to take root and grow. Passion is single focused and committed with a pinpoint target in view. It is mutually exclusive and overcomes all obstacles, while displaying strong emotions that are compelling, like love and hate. It acts with confidence and has the ability to take large risks, even risking rejection. Dopamine gives us the ability to stay focused and on target toward what we want. When someone is passionate about someone, they will usually pursue them at any cost. This is dramatically displayed in many fairy tales, as the hero or heroine passionately pursues their love, despite the dangers and villains they encounter.

Sam Walton of Walmart noted, "I think I overcame every single one of my personal shortcomings by the sheer passion I brought to my work. I don't know if you're born with this kind of passion, or if you can learn it. But I do know you need it. . . . If you love your work, you will be out there every day trying to do it the best you possibly can, and pretty soon everybody around you will catch the passion from you—like a fever."

Passion demands sacrifice, it inspires and is contagious, and when it gets a hold of you, you give all you have. Confident, passionate risks (CPR) revive and restore weary relationships and give you the ability to overcome great odds.

3. Create adventure by connecting.

This sounds easier than it really is for one reason—men and women often connect differently:

- Women bond through secrets, while men bond through competition.
- Women connect through words, using about three times as many words in a day compared to men.
- Women connect through collaboration, where men often connect through hierarchy.
- Women tend to thrive on the bonding hormone oxytocin, while men tend to thrive on adrenaline.
- Women marry for a best friend, while men marry for a recreational partner.

While dating, we play nicely by accommodating each other and participating in activities and conversations we would normally avoid.

But after we've been together for a while, it's not uncommon for us to relax into our own comfort zones and miss cues for attachment.

For years Jenn would invite me (Jake) to join her for Saturday morning breakfast.

I often responded by saying, "Breakfast is the easiest meal to fix at home. Why go out when we can make it easily ourselves?" Who could argue with that logic!

One day Jenn, exasperated, said, "Don't you know why I'm asking you to breakfast? I'm trying to connect with you!"

This is what is called by attachment theorists as a missed cue for attachment, or what marriage expert John Gottman calls a missed bid for connection. Jenn kept asking me for breakfast to spend time with me, talk with me, share with me—and I kept turning her down. Not because I didn't want to connect, but because I wrongly assumed her invitation to me was just about food.

Because men and women connect differently, it's easy to misread our invitations to each other. And whether intentional or not, repeated denials of a bid for connection causes a partner to feel rejected and unimportant—and puts the relationship in danger of alienation.

Eventually partners who feel rejected stop asking for what they want, and resentment can fester in the relationship.

So how do we keep that from happening?

How can we intentionally choose to connect with our partner—in ways that mean something to them?

Understand the power of adrenaline and oxytocin.

So if men thrive with adrenaline, then women thrive with the bonding hormone oxytocin. When women have an inflow of oxytocin, this provides them with more energy, whereas conversely, oxytocin with men relaxes them and causes them to fall asleep. Bonding behaviors such as play, romance, touch, laughter, sex, deep breathing, and eye contact increase oxytocin levels in the body, which in turn enables people to connect and bond.

Travel in the Royal Carriage.

When we were dating in college, we used to love to run the stadium stairs, then end our time together with talking, sharing, prayer, and some smooching. They were rich nights as we connected in all four primary areas of intimacy: physical, emotional, spiritual, and relational.

We call this riding in the Royal Carriage. Picture a carriage with four wheels. Each one has a different purpose in moving the carriage forward: the physical wheel, the emotional wheel, the spiritual wheel, and the relational wheel. Then the horse named Passion is what pulls the carriage down the road.

As corny as this may seem, the picture works for demonstrating the value of having all four wheels engaged for the carriage to move forward. If one wheel is nonexistent or damaged, progress for the relationship moving forward will be limited and challenging.

Like the fairy tale *Beauty and the Beast*, it was difficult for them to connect until they shared some playful courting, shared their hearts with each other, and experienced an adventure together. Their efforts ended with the memorable ball dance in the beautiful enchanted castle ballroom. All efforts to get Belle to fall in love with him in his beastly state would have been futile if he hadn't learned to talk with her, eat politely with her, learn civil communication instead of expressing beastly behavior, and give her beautiful gifts to demonstrate his affection for her. This is something we do organically when we are trying to win the heart of someone. Keeping this connection going is critical to creating adventure with your partner.

Invest time.

Love is spelled t-i-m-e. Years into their relationship, couples often expect the same results from ten minutes spent together compared to the many hours when they first met, playing together, talking for endless hours, and dating till the wee hours of the morning. Intimacy comes easy and naturally in the beginning, and this is what seasoned couples usually want to get back in their relationship.

Unfortunately, our investment in our relationship is often minimal, yet we often expect exceptional results. Adventure rarely happens, and resentment sets in due to unmet, unrealistic expectations from both partners. When a couple learns to spend the time necessary to connect in all four areas, the friendship is nurtured and beacons intimacy to approach with speed.

Give to each other.

Sharing our resources emotionally, physically, and financially provides meaningful connection with one another. When we give—time, play, compliments, our bodies, affection, love, etc.—connection is the natural result. Connection sets a beautiful landscape for intimacy to flourish.

Play with each other.

Playful partners usually do more flirting and have a stronger friendship. Learn to play together and find activities so you can enjoy one another. Date often and bask in the warmth of having someone to play and laugh with. Go out on the town, play games, and remember to laugh with one another.

Affirm your partner for who they are and how they are different from you.

Operate according to your strengths versus the qualities of your gender and how others have stereotyped you to act. Have realistic expectations of one another, and the trust will develop as the connection stays consistent and realistic.

Develop rituals together.

Develop rituals, or patterned behaviors, that you enjoy together to keep your relationship connected and secure. One couple we know, dear friends of ours, goes out every Saturday morning for a Starbucks date. They rehash their week, take time to enjoy the start of the weekend, and just connect. Another couple we know does yoga twice a week together.

Doing the same activity at the same time can also be a connecting experience. Having a predictable behavior creates security and assists in developing a secure attachment.

Stop hiding.

When trust has been broken in a relationship, the best way to restore the fractured trust is to create a positive connection.

One husband used drugs for years without his wife knowing. She was heartbroken and questioned who her husband was and who she married. Meticulously and carefully, he had to learn how to connect with her again instead of using his energy to hide from her.

The result was that she experienced a deeper, more real relationship than she had ever experienced before. Even though the trust had been broken, the greater heartache was the fuzzy connection they had experienced throughout their relationship because he was avoiding connecting with her in an effort to hide his secret from her. When they learned to have a stronger, clearer connection, trust developed and the relationship was elevated to a more satisfying experience.

Although she was hurt by his deceit, she was able to forgive and reconcile with him because the connection became more rewarding than it had ever been before.

When we connect in a healthy way, we create adventure with magical characteristics that enable us to overlook a multitude of hurts and disappointments.

Choose God.

Not only do we long to be chosen by each other to do adventure with, but God longs to be chosen and to create and enjoy adventure with you as well. When we choose God and engage with the spiritual dimension in our relationship with Him, he will help us choose our partner and create adventure with us.

He's our "magic"—the supernatural in our fairy tale—and he created us to connect with him.

Attachment theorists have learned that it is not enough just to connect with people around us. They claim we are hardwired to connect with God *and* each other. This is why every ethnic group through time has had a language, culture, and religion. We are spiritual beings designed to connect spiritually with each other and the Divine.

In your quest to meet the "Choose me!" longing in the heart of your spouse and in your own heart as well, we encourage you to create adventure by having a shared quest. That shared quest should involve mutual interests, taking risks with confidence and passion, and connecting with each other and God. May your longing to be chosen above all others be fulfilled as you choose to create adventure with your partner.

REFLECTION

Describe why you fell in love with your partner.

Rate the amount of adventure in your relationship (circle one):

1 2 3 4 5 6 7 8 9 10

Empty Full

List a few ways you pursued your partner when you first met:

❶

❷

❸

Describe how you can continually choose your partner.

4

PURPLE MEADOWS

After their royal wedding, the prince and princess set out to establish their kingdom. With great anticipation they traveled into the unknown, filled with hope and faith. They had never been outside the walls of their own kingdoms, so a purple kingdom built with blue and pink was thrilling. As they discovered new things about one another, the prince and princess loved every purple detail, merging blue and pink and enjoying the uniqueness of their partner. Playfully, they cherished all of the quirks and imperfections, selflessly considering the wants and needs of the other. The future was bright and exciting. From sunup to sundown the love-struck pair enjoyed their companionship and grew ever deeper in unity. Purple abounded as they recognized that together they were stronger. Dreams and destiny were taking shape.

PART ONE: NAVIGATING THE PURPLE MEADOWS

The chase is over and your love is official. Your lover can do no wrong, and you're both selflessly serving each other and appreciating your differences. Wouldn't it be great to stay here forever?

As we navigate the Purple Meadows, we're going to explore three aspects:

- **The Heart Longing** most deeply felt at this destination *("Appreciate me!")*
- **The Crisis** that threatens your success *(Not Being Appreciated)*
- **The Key** to meeting this heart longing *(Make Purple)*

The Heart Longing: "Appreciate Me!"

We all long to be enjoyed, appreciated, and recognized for what we excel in. We crave affirmation and recognition of our strengths. We want our opinions, talents, and contributions to be enjoyed and appreciated. Pink wants to be appreciated by blue, and blue wants to be appreciated by pink.

It's no surprise Hallmark makes a killing off their attempt to help consumers meet this longing through cards of appreciation on Mother's Day, Father's Day, Valentine's Day, Boss's Day, Secretary's Day, Veterans Day, etc. All have the intent of expressing appreciation to the people we love and what they have given to us.

Showing appreciation through gestures and expressions of gratitude is what makes us excel as humans.

Scientists have recently discovered that it's not just human beings who like to be appreciated. Water also fares better when appreciated. They photographed water molecules before and after a person said "Thank you" to the water, and the transformation was astounding. Before the water was thanked, it looked disorganized and discolored, but after the water was thanked, it looked clear and resembled beautiful, crystallized snowflakes.[2] Since our bodies are made up of more than 70 percent water, how much health could we bring to our lives and relationships if we chose to express appreciation to them?

When I (Jenn) worked at Lourdes Hospital, I was recommended by my fellow employees to receive the Employee of the Month award. I remember being so touched to have the staff and administration recognize me for my hard work through a simple token of a coffee cup with the company logo on it. To be applauded, praised, and appreciated for a job well-done was of far more significance to me than the coffee cup. The simple act of coming together to express gratitude and appreciation for a fellow employee was a gift that still cheers my heart on today.

During my years as a pastor, I (Jake) attended a men's event at the Seattle King Dome (where the Seahawks used to play) called Promise Keepers. At one point during the event, all the pastors in the stadium were asked to come down to the field to receive a standing ovation for their work as ministers. I remember my eyes brimmed with tears as over seventy thousand men cheered and applauded us pastors as loud as they could. The noise and praise were overwhelmingly deafening and caused our spirits to soar as they set a new record that day for reaching the highest decibel level ever recorded at the King Dome (even louder than the Seattle Seahawks games). Now that's appreciation!

We may not all be able to experience that kind of expression, but rest assured, when we are thanked and appreciation is expressed, it is always a gift to our spirits. Will Rogers said, "We can't all be heroes because someone has to sit on the curb and clap as they go by." We say, "Let's take turns being heroes for each other and clap for each other as the other passes by."

One husband we counseled showed appreciation for his wife in a unique way. Whenever she would go out to eat, she loved to have a glass of iced tea sweetened with Equal. But he noticed on many occasions she would have to use a substitute sweetener since they wouldn't have her preferred brand. So he began the treasured habit of carrying Equal packets in his breast pocket for her.

Every time they went out to eat, he would save the day by pulling the little Equal packets out of his pocket. He treated her like a queen by carrying Equal packets for her and showing appreciation for what was important to her.

C.S. Lewis emphasizes this point in the following quote: "I think we delight to praise what we enjoy because the praise not merely expresses but completes the enjoyment. It is not out of compliment that lovers keep on telling one another how beautiful they are; the delight is incomplete till it is expressed." We need to express appreciation for one another in order to meet a very basic longing of us all.

The Crisis: Not Being Appreciated

When we are overlooked, passed over, and not appreciated for what we have to give, we begin to feel defeated. When we are ignored, run over, and not enjoyed, we start wondering if we are important, if we have anything valuable to offer our partner.

Pink and blue kingdoms start competing instead of appreciating each other. We lose focus of our purpose on this planet, and it becomes blurry as we seek to be enjoyed or noticed by one another instead of being filled up to seek our greater purpose.

We fight to get our color, or our kingdom, noticed, which we refer to as "color bullying," and we attempt to impose our needs on each other. We look elsewhere if we don't get recognized, and our attentions shift to another who is quick to praise and flower us with appreciation.

It is not surprising how often affairs start with the sheer power of the expression of appreciation through compliments. One man I (Jenn) counseled had an affair on his wife when the other woman kept encouraging him and complimenting him at his work. His wife repeatedly attacked his career choice and work progress, and often criticized him for the hours he worked, instead of expressing appreciation for what he provided for her. Often, we hear how women enjoy their friends more than their spouse or how husbands enjoy hunting more than being with their wife. When there is appreciation consistently coming from your partner, it is hard to choose anything other than your partner. This heart longing to be appreciated is so strong, it will make a relationship that excels in it and break a relationship that is void of it.

Here's a chilling story of the ultimate crisis that occurs when appreciation is absent:

"Carlyle had a very devoted wife who sacrificed everything for his sake, but he never gave her a single expression of appreciation for which her heart yearned. She came to regard herself as the most miserable woman in London and evidently died of heart hunger. After her death, Carlyle, reading her diary, realized the truth. A friend found him at her grave suffering intense remorse and exclaiming, 'If I had only known!'"[3]

Now is the time to tell.

Withholding appreciation from our loved one is another way to enact revenge or hurt them, intentionally or unintentionally. Our hearts were not designed to live without being appreciated and will wither without the powerful fuel of appreciation.

The Key: Make Purple

When we learn to really appreciate each other, we are then capable to blend who we are with one another. In One Kingdom, we call this principle "making purple," where the blue kingdom blends with the pink kingdom to make purple.

Although as men and women we all have the same longings, heterosexual couples can really struggle with this concept due to the distinct differences between the genders. John Grey humorously demonstrated these differences with his popular book *Men Are from Mars, Women Are from Venus*. The title says it all: men and women are from two different planets, with different languages and cultures. No wonder frustration and confusion abound!

Appreciation is the precursor to making purple with your partner. Let's explore some concrete and clear ways to create a healthy, mutual connection with your partner from another planet.

PART TWO:
YOUR QUEST IN THE PURPLE MEADOWS

In order to make purple, your marriage has to answer three questions:

1. *Where* did we come from?
2. *Who* are we as a couple?
3. *What* are we here for?

Here's how to do that:

1. Make purple by appreciating pink and blue.

When you both appreciate pink and blue, you answer the question, "Where did we come from?"

When we appreciate what each has to offer, we blend the strengths of the pink and the blue kingdoms and we make the royal hue of purple. We take the best of each and make royalty, and it is no coincidence that purple is commonly known as the color of royalty. We can make purple by appreciating pink and blue!

It is important, but not always easy, to appreciate each other's kingdom. We know this does not come as a big surprise to most, but men and women come from two very different kingdoms. And like any other kingdom, each has its own culture, vision, language, values, fashion, and approaches to life that are entirely different from their partner's kingdom. What seems like a no-brainer to one is not even on the radar for the other kingdom.

Early on in our marriage, I (Jake) remember learning this lesson vividly as I was driving my new bride up to the Pacific Northwest from Southern California. I still remember gripping the steering wheel in tense frustration, internally dialoguing with myself, "If I can just learn to tolerate her differences, I may have a shot at succeeding at this thing called marriage."

Then it was as if the heavens opened up and I had this revolutionary truth revealed to me: I needed to learn to appreciate Jenn, not just tolerate her. It was as if I was freed up to become a student of her instead of gritting through tolerating her. It was a pivotal moment in our marriage as I realized my job was to appreciate Jenn and the pink kingdom she originated from, who spoke *way* too many words and had something to say about *everything*. Ahhh, appreciating her brought a refreshing air to the stale state of tolerance.

Many fairy tales highlight and often capitalize on the contrasting differences of the prince and princess. We see a stark contrast in Ariel the mermaid, who lived in the ocean, while Prince Eric was a man who lived on land. We can't get much different in culture than that! Wonder what a therapy session would be like for the two of them learning to appreciate their differences. We can hear it now:

> **Ariel.** "Do you know what I gave up for you?! My mermaid life and tail!"
>
> **Prince Eric**. "No really, I can't visit your family ever!! I'm not just trying to be difficult. It will kill me!"

Or what about Cinderella and Prince Charming? That was quite a step up in culture for Miss Cinderella. She went from sweeping the fireplaces in rags to dancing around fireplaces in gowns. From being ordered around to being the one giving orders. The ashes that crowned her head were replaced with jewels embedded in a crown. This was quite the contrast from the life she left, compared to the privileged life of her prince. I'm sure there were some adjustment difficulties on the prince's part in accommodating his less than charming new in-laws. These two couples alone would have kept us busy with therapy in helping them learn to appreciate their uniqueness and contrasting traits. Our differences are often why we fall in love. We are attracted to the uniqueness of another even though this often becomes what we fight about later.

One couple, when asked how they were doing in their marriage, looked at us and said, "We are making purple." They were learning to make purple when it came to their communication. She had been talking and sharing a lot, and he been sharing little. He had to learn to communicate more and her less so they could enjoy their marriage.

Another man went through a spiritual transformation and ended up changing his religious beliefs. He spent over two years studying his religion, never telling his wife, and when she finally discovered this, she was hurt and shocked. After some counseling about the importance of sharing him with her and how it makes her feel close to him, they were sent home to attempt to bridge the gap from him to her. At the next session, she commented on how good their marriage had become and how close they felt. When the husband was asked how it was going for him, he said confidently, "We're making purple."

These two couples are learning to change the landscape of their relationship by appreciating, nurturing, and enjoying the pink kingdom and the blue kingdom. By merging the two kingdoms, the two are becoming One Kingdom, full of the strength and beauty of each. This is easy when you're just starting out and your partner is "perfect." As time goes on and you come to see the true flaws and imperfections of your partner, the quest to make purple in your relationship can be more challenging. In order to create oneness, we need to leave our own kingdoms, cling to each other, and rule One Kingdom together. The royal purple design cannot be created unless there is confidence your partner wants you, appreciates you, and wants what you have to offer.

Marriage expert John Gottman says the marriage starts to change in a positive and powerful direction when the man begins to take the influence of his wife. In our work and in our marriage, we find this to be a powerful truth. Women are often encouraged or trained, whether due to nature or nurture from our patriarchal society, to accept the influence of the man. Women are more collaborative and relational by nature, whereas men are more hierarchical and independent by nature. The topic of self-care and nurturing yourself has rarely surfaced in our work with men, but it is a regular topic of concern with women, who tend to feel they must overperform, or overextend themselves, for the sake of their marriage, children, and friendships, bringing themselves in last for nurturance. Men, on the other hand, are naturally skilled at taking care of themselves, despite the discomfort this would bring to their relationships, so they don't often feel the need to discuss it in counseling. The term "golf widow" and women's expressions of fear and abandonment as hunting season rolls around point to the skill men have in being single focused in taking care of themselves.

This might be men's greatest strength but also their greatest weakness. To take care of one's self in spite of how it may hurt others can be a strength, but to do this without learning to appreciate one's wife can have devastating results. Women start becoming resentful that their needs and feelings are not being appreciated, and they may become aggressive in getting their needs met. This is where the "nagging wife" comes in, and they both begin the bullying process to get what they need for themselves or their family. We often see the woman advocating for her children or the needs of the family before she advocates for herself, whereas the man is clamoring for his personal needs, such as hunting, biking, running, golf, work, etc.—in other words, his need to thrive.

Research experts for nonprofits have found that for every dollar a woman earns she invests eighty cents in her family, whereas men invest thirty cents into the family and are more likely to squander money on alcohol or other vices. Researchers found if they can empower the women, they will best assist the families in crisis.[4] Men are skilled in nurturing themselves, which in turn gives them the ability to provide best for their families—if they are good-hearted. If not, we find they use their ability to care for themselves as their primary goal, often using their marriage and family to provide for their wounded ego.

We encourage women to learn from men's strength in being passionately self-nurturing and for men to learn from women's strength in being passionately self-sacrificing. Like men, women's greatest strength and greatest weakness—nurturing—becomes severely out of balance when they nurture everyone else besides themselves. When this happens, a wife will get resentful of their partner, who is taking care of himself and keeping himself happy through his activities. Women often struggle to unhook from the marriage and family, even placing the responsibility of self-nurturance on their partner. This is often where the nagging and criticism come in. A burned-out, depressed, unfulfilled woman is a lackluster wife or mother. No one wins when the woman allows all of her divine nurturance to go out to others and leaves none for herself, then goes around blaming and criticizing her partner for taking care of himself and not her. This pattern often drives the man to take care of himself even more, as he feels attacked by his wife, driving the wife into further resentment and depression. We need to appreciate each other's differences and learn to make purple when it comes to sharing our resources in order to best care for ourselves, our marriage, and our family.

One couple had this familiar conflict when the husband insisted on going hunting for three months of the year. Before marrying, they both agreed to this, and it wasn't much of a problem for the wife until children came along. She began to feel neglected and bitter as he went off on his hunting trips, leaving her to care for their small infant. He reminded her, this is what you married and told her this before they married. She felt resigned to accept her fate, and found herself becoming less in love with her husband and more resentful toward him. A miserable partnership had evolved, thus bringing them to therapy. When she was able to hear how his hunting kept him alive, passionate, and it didn't mean he loved her less, she softened toward his needs. Then when he could hear that she wanted him to have his hunting, but she also wanted more family and connection time with him, he stopped misinterpreting her "nagging" as control and saw it more as a means to connect with him. I (Jenn) sent them off with the assignment to "make purple" in their differences by appreciating each other's needs and perspectives. At the next session, they came in more peaceful and affectionate, as they announced they were able to make purple in their differences. He agreed to reduce his hunt down to a month a year, then take some weekend trips with her and the baby hunting and camping. (Note: This compromise worked since she happened to enjoy hunting and camping. Not all women would find this to be an agreeable compromise.) She was also encouraged to take up some hobbies and spend time with her friends while he spent more time watching the baby. They agreed it was not an easy process but well worth the time. He was tired of living with an unhappy, depressed, resentful wife, and she was unhappy feeling unheard, unappreciated, and alone. Making purple with compromising and appreciating each other's differences was a worthy alternative to the life they were living and the path they were on.

Besides the self-care difference, we find another huge difference men and women have a difficult time appreciating is the emotional versus logical approaches women and men take, respectively. I (Jake) come from a highly logical, no-nonsense family, where making decisions based on what makes sense and can be logically deduced as being the best and most efficient decision ruled supremely. Enter Jenn, a highly sensitive person who would often make very sound decisions just because it did or didn't "feel" right. She could rarely give reasons for her decisions, but she often made great decisions when it came to people, relationships, business adventures, child-raising, and more. As someone who values logic, I had a hard time appreciating Jenn's decision-making process based mainly on feeling. Because of this, many conflicts ensued, and Jenn often ended up giving in to my perspective because of her inability to provide logic for her opinions.

This was dramatically displayed when we were building our home. We both met with the hardwood floor installer at his office, who promised to sell us beautiful wood flooring at a great price. After meeting with him, I (Jenn) simply said, "There is something not right with him," and decided I did not want to do business with him. To Jake, this didn't make sense, but he appreciated my feeling and decided to check out references elsewhere. Everyone else said he checked out fine and had been in business in our small town for over twenty years. I still felt uneasy about him but could not give any reason why. I ended up doubting myself and agreed to do business with him. Weeks went by with no floor product delivered, and I continued to feel uneasy, like he was lying to us. Jake appreciated my apprehension and did a background check on him. Come to find out, he was under investigation for tax evasion, and his business license had been revoked! He was robbing from us to pay back other clients, as he had gotten in over his head financially. It was an expensive ($7,000) loss and a painful lesson we learned. To appreciate each other's differences and how we make decisions may not always make sense, but it can save us many a heartache when we learn to appreciate both emotional and logical approaches to decision making. (Side note: Jake ended up patiently building a relationship with the floor guy and eventually got him to pay back all our money!)

We have countless examples of this in our marriage and the marriages we've worked with, where one partner overrides the apprehension and concern of the other partner because they are so intent on getting what they want. Then when they push and bully to get what they want without appreciating their partner's viewpoint, they often find less than satisfying results or devastating consequences for their decision to press forward without the support and peace of their partner. It saddens us when we see couples move from appreciating each other to overriding one another and using God as their reason for the power play. As if it is men's divine right to "take authority over their wife" or "make the final decision" in conflicted decisions, despite the protests of their partner. We encourage couples to move forward in peace in their decision making, accepting the strengths of each and appreciating what each brings to the table in the process.

It is hard to appreciate each other if you don't know yourself enough to teach your partner about you. Here are a few simple personality tests you can take to discover more of who you are and the uniqueness of your partner:

- Color Code Personality Test (www.colorcode.com/personality_test)
- VIA Survey of Character Strengths (www.authentichappiness.sas.upenn.edu/testcenter)
- Animal Personality Test (https://www.mint-hr.com/smalley-trent.html)
- Riso-Hudson Enneagram Type Indicator (https://www.enneagraminstitute.com or www.9types.com/rheti/index.php)

Make purple by appreciating pink and blue and the unique characteristics of each. This makes for a powerful blend we call One Kingdom, which emits a beautiful royal purple hue.

2. Make purple in your kingdom design.

When you make purple in your kingdom design, you answer the question: "Who are we as a couple?"

Appreciate each other by developing shared values, vision, and strategy to implement your kingdom design. Learn to merge your two individual kingdoms into a purple kingdom.

Remember those adventure books where you could choose how the story was going to go, the Choose Your Own Adventure books? The author would bring you to a climactic part in the story, then ask you to choose if you want "Bill to enter the haunted house, turn to page 47" or "Bill to explore the dark forest, turn to page 58." It felt powerful to choose the direction of the book and to dictate what the characters did. We get to do that in our relationships if we want. We get to choose how we talk, interact, bond, and act with our partner, and we get to determine where we are headed as a couple. The greatest challenge in hitting a target is setting what that target is. You may not hit the bull's-eye every time, but you will hit somewhere on or near the target if you're pointing toward it. Relationships are no different. There needs to be a target you are *both* aiming at in order to get the greatest success from your partnership.

Marriages fall apart when there are unmet expectations, and this is the most common reason couples divorce. One couple we worked with had appeared to start off with a similar target in mind, but as time went on, either the target shifted for one partner, or there never was the compatibility they once believed they had. She was the administrator of a school, living a public life that would not allow her to compromise her integrity. Although he started off as a reputable business man in the community, he became addicted to drugs and pornography, then dramatically ended their several-decade marriage by running off with the woman he had an affair with. This was a conflict of vision, which created a conflicted life as a couple. They were aiming at two different targets, and in the end, the arrows turned toward each other.

Sound familiar? We've all heard a story like this, or you may be one who has lived it. Having similar expectations and vision for the marriage is imperative to creating a successful partnership. We see marriage or relationships like a business that needs a good vision statement to be successful, and we use a three-step process with our couples to accomplish this.

1. Establish Core Values
2. Develop a Marriage Vision Statement
3. Create a Marriage Strategy

If businesses expect to have successful mergers and partnerships, and to meet strategy goals around working cohesively and effectively together, how much *more* do marriages and partnerships with people from two entirely different kingdoms need this three-step process? We believe there are too many unrealistic expectations and myths surrounding marriage that are contributing to the failure of too many "kingdom mergers," or marriages and committed relationships. Like businesses, couples need to first establish what their core values are so they can make purple in their One Kingdom.

1. Establish Core Values

Within the corporate world, it is common for companies to establish core values. Values can be defined as something you give worth to that assists in guiding your life and what you use your resources for. For instance, Starbucks's core values include community service, ecofriendliness, and third world aid. Volvo's primary core value is safety, and they place such a high value or worth on safety, all their decisions are based on the question, "Does this provide safety for the consumer?" Therefore, they are known for being one of the safest cars on the road by the car industry and consumers. Walmart's core value is "Everyday Low Prices," which is reflected in the affordable prices of their products.

In our own marriage, our core values are love, inspiration, validation, equity, play, and comfort. When you establish your core values, you create the culture of your relationship. These values guide your decisions and life choices.

2. Develop a Marriage Vision Statement

Similarly, all successful companies have a vision statement, stating who they are as a company and where they are going. If you want to be a power couple with common direction and goals in life, create a vision statement. Know where you are going as a couple, and stay committed, both individually and together, to exacting the vision you create for your marriage. A good vision statement can take years to create as it is tweaked, corrected, changed, and improved upon.

There are several components of an effective vision statement: clear, concise, action inspiring, and future focused. For instance, Starbucks's vision statement is "To inspire and nurture the human spirit—one person, one cup and one neighborhood at a time." To create your marriage vision statement, begin with "Our marriage is . . . ," then incorporate your core values as a couple in a sentence or two. For example, our own vision statement reads, "Our marriage is an intimate partnership, centered on God, filled with love, play, freedom, and passion; it is a supportive, safe, and dynamic relationship nurtured through trust, compassion, and affirmation to provide energy to live happily and inspire others."

3. Create a Marriage Strategy

It is one thing to have a beautiful marriage vision statement, but it is another thing to live it. This is the application part, how you as a couple are going to make this vision happen in your relationship.

We like to be a little corny and tell couples that if they want their relationship to be "DWMY" (pronounced *dweamy*, aka "dreamy"), they need to have a Daily, Weekly, Monthly, Yearly strategy to accomplish their vision.

For instance, one couple we worked with drew apart due to a life-threatening illness the wife had. The husband was terrified and pulled away from the wife, leaving her alone to battle the horrific disease alone. Because of this, she found comfort in another man.

Through much grief and pain, they were able to understand their parts in the demise of their marriage. After much work, they came up with the following DWMY plan:

Daily share about their days, pray together, and eat one meal together.
Weekly go out on dates and watch their favorite show.
Monthly go out to breakfast and share how they are doing in their marriage and staying connected, as well as attend a monthly marriage therapy session.
Yearly go to their favorite vacation spot and spend time enjoying each other, as well as attend a marriage workshop or read a relationship improvement book.

Decide as a couple what you want to do to keep your relationship alive and growing. Create a DWMY plan together, and both make a commitment to follow the plan. It is common for one person to be in charge of nurturing the relationship, which can cause some resentment and relationship fatigue. This was the case in our relationship, so we like to split up the days of the week and each of us be in charge of certain days to initiate nurturing the DWMY plan. Here is an example of one of our plans:

Jake takes Tuesdays and Thursdays.
Jenn takes Wednesdays and Fridays.
Mondays are a shared day set aside to nurture each other (since Mondays are the hardest day of the week for us after coming off the weekend).
Saturdays are our date night. Jake takes first and third Saturdays of the month, and Jenn takes the second and fourth Saturdays of the month to plan the dates.

Caring for a marriage or relationship can be compared to caring for a child. It requires constant care and skilled conflict management for it to develop and mature. If we allow resentment, bitterness, and fear to replace acceptance, grace, and love, we can arrest the development of the marriage, thus providing a toxic or deflating environment for our souls. It is our responsibility to feed and care for our marriage so it can grow up to be a mature, nurturing entity that can support our spirits. This must be a shared responsibility of both partners to achieve admirable results.

3. Make purple by blending your purpose.

When you blend your purpose, you answer the question, "What are we here for?"

Finally, appreciate each other by blending your purpose. Purpose is best defined as "the impact you have on others." The happiest people in the world live with purpose, and experts promote how purpose gives longevity to your life.

It is impossible to blend if you are unsure of your individual purpose, much less the purpose of the relationship. Before you attempt to establish your relationship purpose, take some time to ask yourself, "What is my purpose, and what is the impact I want to have on others?" You may already know this, or you may need to dwell on this for a time. It is common for one partner to have a stronger understanding of their purpose than another, but it is essential that both establish their own personal purpose to make a strong purple blend of their relationship purpose.

One couple we knew learned the hard way what happens when you don't take the time to understand your own purpose and the relationship purpose. She married him because he was cute, they were attracted to each other, and the sex was good. He married her because she was attractive, energetic, and a good lover. But after twenty-five years of marriage, two kids, and numerous cheating incidents by him, he confessed he never loved her. Their children were grown, which had become their only purpose together, and the expiration date of the marriage was up. They were over. Instead of choosing to recreate a new purpose together, they chose to terminate their marriage and date other people. Creating a purpose for your marriage adds longevity to your relationship and gives it a long shelf life, with no expiration date. Kind of like a Twinkie that has no expiration date because it is so jam packed with preservatives. Purpose preserves the relationship and provides longevity.

We can see the power of blending purposes in companies. For example, consider the Bill and Melinda Gates Foundation and various pharmaceutical companies coming together to fight malaria. The Gateses have always been about building computer software but have added a new vision together of attacking issues worldwide that cause hardships in third world countries. Through their combined resources and vision, their worldwide impact has been astounding and inspiring.

Deaths caused by malaria have dropped 38 percent, with forty-three countries cutting the number of malaria cases in half.

One million children's lives have been saved from malaria.

One-third of countries affected by malaria are now on track to eliminate the disease.

Our shared purpose in our counseling practice is derived and inspired from the Bible passage Isaiah 61:1–3. This passage describes how Jesus came to bind up the brokenhearted, give freedom to those who are captive to darkness, and bring comfort and joy to those who mourn. This scripture sits on our desks as a constant reminder of what we are about in our work. We want to assist people in experiencing freedom from guilt, shame, fear, and abuse; to understand and guide them in their healing process; and to share truths and insights that complement a life of freedom and health. Unity and equity help to heal relationships and provide good soil for love and grace to take root in a hopeless relationship. We help individuals look at their three primary relationships with God, self, and others, and how to get the optimum experience from life as they keep these relationships healthy and nurtured. This is what guides our practice and has kept us going for over twenty years in a field that usually has a seven-year burnout term. Without purpose, it would be easy for us to get lost in the despair and deep pain of others with no relief for any of us.

The value of having purpose beyond ourselves, where we are not just focused on our own happiness and needs, is critical to having a fulfilling life. Positive psychologists find that the happiest and most successful people have purpose, a deliberate impact on others, and as a result, they are more engaged and connected to others. We are designed for a bigger purpose that goes beyond our marriage and family, and God brought us together for a bigger reason. It is your responsibility to discover that and make purple as you live your shared purpose as a couple. As one father told his son, "Just go for it and give it a try! You don't have to be a professional to build a successful product. Amateurs started Google and Apple. Professionals built the Titanic." There is no one perfect couple with one perfect purpose. We are all on our relationship journeys at different stages and with different hurdles to overcome. And you are the expert on yourself and your relationship. Setting a target and giving it a good try will move you somewhere near the target. Go for it, and remember perfection is never the goal; progress is.

Men and women need to take the time to fully appreciate each other so they can make purple in their partnership. Also, it is impossible to fully appreciate your partner if you are not appreciating yourself and what your kingdom has to offer both of you. To make purple with your partner does not mean for the pink kingdom or blue kingdom to be eliminated, but rather for both to be developed and drawn from so you can make the royal purple One Kingdom. Take the time to nurture and develop yourself, appreciating your differences, strengths, and weaknesses, so you can best appreciate your partner.

REFLECTION

What are some of your partner's and your own unique strengths?

List a few differences that complement your partner:

BLUE PINK

❶

❷

❸

Mark where your relationship currently resides on the "Purple continuum":

Pink -------------------Purple -------------------Blue

What is your blended purpose as a couple (i.e., impact on others)?

List the top five core values for your relationship (e.g., fun, passion, joy):

1.

2.

3.

4.

5.

Create a simple vision statement for your relationship incorporating the most important core values and *purpose* of your relationship.

Our marriage is . . .

Begin to develop a marriage strategy with practical objectives that will help you accomplish your vision and purpose.

Daily:

Weekly:

Monthly:

Yearly:

5

DARK FOREST

Without warning, the prince and princess wandered into a deep, dark forest. Their peace was overthrown by confusion, and their joy masked by shadows. They were not alone in this dark forest, as thieves and villains lurked in the twisted darkness, waiting for an opportunity to strike. Fearful and vulnerable, the two began to fight frequently, somehow seeing the other as the enemy. They swung their swords and slung arrows in confusion, carelessly wounding one another. Neither knew which way to turn, and they blamed each other for this place of misfortune. With trust quickly fading, the prince and princess grew ever more callous and hard-hearted, quickly losing sight of the deep romance they shared. The weakened couple would have to learn to cast out fear and shame, and fight together to survive as one. Desperate for a place to rest and heal, the royal couple noticed a light through the trees and moved desperately toward it.

PART ONE: NAVIGATING THE DARK FOREST

The perfect romance is blindsided by conflict and sudden darkness. Every relationship encounters it, and it leaves you wounded, bitter, and vulnerable. It's vital that you learn how to fight together for your love's survival.

As we navigate the Dark Forest, we're going to explore three aspects:

- **The Heart Longing** most deeply felt at this destination ("*Protect Me!"*)
- **The Crisis** that threatens your success *(Not Being Protected)*
- **The Key** to meeting this heart longing *(Fight Fairly)*

The Heart Longing: "Protect Me!"

One Kingdom is established and maintained when the elements of protection are present. The heart longing of this destination is simply this: "Protect me!"

There is nothing like the feeling of being protected, of relaxing in the knowledge that another person has your back. When someone is committed to protecting you, you feel valued and cherished. You live and love more confidently, without fear of abandonment, knowing you will never be forced to defend and protect yourself alone.

For men, we're talking about your wingman. The guy who has your back when you approach a girl to ask her out or when the love of your life has just broken your heart.

For women, we're talking about your BFF. The friend to whom you tell all your secrets. The person you do pedicures with. The bestie who always give you a shoulder to cry on when life takes a crazy turn.

These loyal friends can tell you like it is and get away with it because you know that, ultimately, they have your best interest at heart. You know they will stay with you, protect you, and fight with you and for you, no matter what.

The longing to feel protected is innate. In fact, research shows that when babies are not protected or cared for, it changes the way their brains are wired, and they can struggle to attach successfully for the rest of their lives. This is because overdeveloped survival skills are taking all their emotional resources and preventing them from successfully navigating critical developmental stages of life.

As adults, we are just babies grown big, and we need to feel protected too. When we feel protected and nurtured, we are empowered to use our emotional resources to develop ourselves instead of protecting ourselves. When we feel protected and nurtured, we can thrive instead of merely survive.

Both men and women have this intense need to be protected.

Women have the need to feel physical protection from their partner. With women and children being the primary victims on this planet, it is very comforting for women to know their partner can do what needs to be done to protect her and the children.

Men need more protection of their character, to know they are respected by their partner. They need to know their character will not be assaulted and they will be valued and honored for who they are. When a man's partner builds him up and shows respect for what he contributes to the relationship, the man feels protected. When he is brutally criticized and condemned for what he does not contribute, his spirit goes into survival mode.

The Crisis: Not Being Protected

Let's take a closer look at what happens when this heart longing isn't met.

When we don't feel protected, we become afraid and our sympathetic nervous system kicks in. As a result, we can experience one or all of these reactions: fight, flight, or freeze. Our brains and bodies feel threatened, so we rally whatever resources we can and become intensely focused on surviving.

Physically, the body quickly redirects resources to keep us alive and kicking. Our hearing decreases, we lose our peripheral vision, and our heart rate increases to over ninety-five beats a minute, all with the intent of keeping us alive. Adrenaline courses through us as the body works courageously and efficiently to give us extra strength for the fight, flight, or freeze we might need to survive.

When our bodies go into survival mode, John Gottman calls this being "flooded." When this happens, our focus on survival hijacks our senses and we can find ourselves doing or saying things we wouldn't normally do or say.

Every year we visit the Oregon Coast. While we were writing this curriculum for One Kingdom, we took our annual trip to Lincoln City, Oregon. As we were approaching the beach on one of the days, we noticed these yellow warning signs for beach visitors. They read "Do Not Feed the Wildlife," "Beware of Rip Currents," etc.

But there was one sign that really caught our attention and our funny bone. It displayed a drawing of a man under a huge wave that was just about to crash down on top of him, with the caption "Watch for Sneaker Waves."

Sneaker wave. What a great illustration of what it feels like to be flooded: a threat has overwhelmed you completely, drowning all your senses and leaving you gasping for air, fighting for your life.

When you get hijacked by a sneaker wave, you're not even thinking clearly. You may sound and act guarded, defensive, critical, and aggressive. You may bully, fight, and stonewall. You may walk out of a confrontation, leaving your partner feeling abandoned.

And when your partner feels abandoned or attacked, guess what? They can feel flooded too. They can go into survival mode and become guarded, defensive, critical, aggressive. They can bully, fight, and stonewall. They can abandon you.

In other words, the very person you thought would protect you becomes the enemy, someone from whom you need to protect yourself.

And vice versa.

This is a terrifying and uncomfortable experience.

One couple who was experiencing a tremendous amount of conflict and considering ending the relationship made a brave attempt at therapy. When the husband was asked why he didn't connect with his wife, he made a subconscious gesture that spoke volumes: he shifted his left arm protectively over his heart.

Then he said, "She hurts me and she never listens to me."

Being a new resident in the country, having left her family and country, she replied, "He hurts me, yet he is all I have to hang onto."

Both exuded the desperation and hurt of not feeling protected by the other.

Of course, one of the most profound experiences of not "feeling protected" by one's partner takes place when that partner has had an affair. The broken trust in a romantic relationship is one of the greatest traumas to recover from, and we believe it is because of the critical need to be protected by a trusted loved one.

When trust is present, this creates safety so the relationship can flourish. When trust is shattered, it sends us tumbling back emotionally. We may even find ourselves regressing in how we express ourselves emotionally. It is not uncommon for the betrayed partner to throw tantrums as they deal with the traumatic reality of not being protected.

Feeling protected by a partner is such a deep need and basic expectation in marriage that when this is shattered, things get messy fast.

In fact, it can create very conflicted feelings as partners attempt to salvage safety and trust, while recovering from the shame each is experiencing in the relationship and still negotiating their commitment and love for the other.

Recovery requires achieving a challenging balance that can take years to navigate.

When we work with couples recovering from a betrayal—infidelity, deceitful behavior, or abandonment—we often see the offended party experience volatile emotions, while the offender experiences a tremendous amount of shame. In other words, both suffer.

One woman described her husband's abandonment of her this way: "I feel like I've lost my home." Although she still loved him, she was emotionally unstable with him since her security in him was shattered.

One man, recovering from his wife's affair, said, "I feel like I'm on an emotional roller coaster, and I hate myself for the hurt it is causing her." Even though her actions had left him unprotected, he still wanted to protect her from the hurt his pain was now bringing her.

In another relationship where verbal abuse was present, the offender, upon realizing the deep wounds he had caused his spouse, said, "I don't know how to forgive myself for the pain I've brought." Both parties were reeling from the lack of protection they either experienced or provided. Because of this, it was easy for both to trigger each other into a flooded state, drowning each other in the fight.

It is also common for a person to feel ashamed when they have not been protected, as if they somehow did something to deserve the betrayal or abuse. When a person betrays the trust of the partner by seeking the attention of another, some might blame the offended partner for not being enough to keep the partner's attention. Likewise, when a partner is verbally and emotionally abusive, it is common for the offended partner to feel as if they did something to deserve how they were treated.

Carl Jung, a famous psychoanalyst, said, "Seldom or never does a marriage develop smoothly and without crisis. There is no birth of consciousness without pain."

Hurtful moments and experiences are inevitable in every relationship. In the process, it's easy to begin seeing each other as the enemy—the villain in our story.

In every story there is a Dark Forest filled with villains and darkness that leave us confused as to how to move forward.

Whatever you may be going through, take hope that there is a key that can help you begin to tame the darkness obscuring the path to your "happily ever after."

The Key: Fight Fairly

The key to escaping the Dark Forest of emotionally abandoning and hurting each other is this: fight fairly.

Dr. Howard Hendricks has said, "People get married with a picture in their minds of a perfect marriage. Then after a few trials, they discover they aren't married to a perfect picture, but an imperfect person. When this realization occurs, they will either tear up the picture or they will tear up the person."[5]

Conflict can be messy. In the Dark Forest, we want you to learn how to partner together to resolve conflict without tearing each other apart. To work together to resolve conflict, move toward the light, and escape the darkness. Perfection is never the goal but rather progress. We believe progress can be made with the presence of conflict as long as we set and follow guidelines for how to fight productively.

PART TWO:
YOUR QUEST IN THE DARK FOREST

Your first assignment is to begin to identify the true villains responsible for your visit to the Dark Forest.

And if you're not *currently* wandering lost in the Dark Forest, don't stop reading. At any stage in your marriage, allowing these villains free reign in your relationship is the fastest way to find yourself in a dark and scary place.

If you identify any of these villains operating in your marriage, send them packing. And the best way to do that is to enlist the help of the corresponding hero.

1. Fight fairly by fighting the villains and inviting the heroes.

Comedian Alan King once said that "marriage is nature's way of keeping people from fighting with strangers." It never ceases to amaze us how easy it is to go from thinking *He/she is perfect for me and can do no wrong* to *I'm married to my enemy.*

This is when many couples walk into our office.

They are tired of fighting each other instead of protecting each other. They are exhausting from tearing at each other's hearts instead of seeking to mend the wounds from within and without. Sometimes people are trying to resolve issues from their childhood by duking it out with their partner in marriage.

Fight fairly by identifying and fighting the real villains in your marriage (hint: it's not your spouse).

In the fairy tale *Beauty and the Beast*, Belle immediately saw a beast who was frightening and cruel. She resisted his advances until she was able to see him for who he truly was, instead of who she initially saw him to be.

To protect your partner, you need to see him or her for who he or she truly is, instead of the cruel beast you imagine them to be. Learn to protect each other by fighting together and not each other. To do this, it is critical that you realize you have a mistaken image of your partner and are fighting the wrong villain.

You need to recognize the real enemy.

Even in fairy tales, if you look closely, the villain is more than meets the eye.

Cinderella's real obstacle was her helplessness, hopelessness, and passivity to a cruel stepmother. She eventually overcame this by daring to dream and reaching beyond her dreary life. With or without the help of a fairy godmother, Cinderella still had to make the risky choice to step beyond the boundaries of her life of cinders to experience a night of magic.

In *Beauty and the Beast*, the villains of fear and imaginary thinking plagued Belle. She had to step outside of her comfortable world and learn to embrace reality instead of escaping reality through books.

Little Red Riding Hood was almost done in by the villains of naïveté, curiosity, and ignorance. When confronted with danger, she didn't run away but hung around studying "Granny's" face and asking questions of the wolf, unable to process or accept reality and get herself to safety.

Who is the villain in your marriage? Is it your spouse? Probably not.

As do fairy tales, our relationships have deeper, more sinister villains that keep us wandering aimlessly and desperately through the Dark Forest. The goal of these villains? To entrap you and confuse you into fighting each other instead of identifying and fighting the *real* enemies of your "happily ever after."

We have identified the top seven deadly villains destroying relationships—and the heroes that can help you escape the clutches of these terrifying yet pathetic villains.

Each villain is listed with a corresponding hero. For example, the first villain/hero pairing is "Fear vs. Love."

Fear vs. Love

Villain: Fear

Where there is fear, love cannot reign. "Perfect love casts out all fear" (1 John 4:18 ESV), and conversely, when we choose to allow fear to reign, love gets banished from our lives and relationships. Broken trust, hurtful treatment, manipulation, deceit, and illness are just a few things that can invite fear to reign in a relationship. We cannot always avoid the hurt we experience or cause in our relationships, but we can choose how to respond to it.

Hero: Love

This is the greatest hero of all. When we love, we operate in a different realm, a realm where forgiveness, empathy, kindness, compassion, understanding, and patience are the languages spoken.

By choosing the language of tenderness, we embrace all of who we are and our spouses are, unconditionally.

While loving others is the superpower that will help us defeat fear, we want to add that we can only love others to the depth we love ourselves. When we learn to love ourselves unconditionally, we learn to love others fearlessly.

Shame vs. Grace

Villain: Shame

Shame is made up of criticism, complaints, contempt, and other messages that say you're "not enough." These shame messages put you in a FOG of fear, obligation, and guilt, and make it difficult for you to lead a productive life. Shame also prevents you from trusting and loving intimately. It is also the cause of conflict and misunderstandings, since shame convinces you that other people are looking for ways to make you feel small.[6]

"Shame and love are grounded in vulnerability and tenderness. . . . If you put shame in a petri dish, it needs three ingredients to grow exponentially: secrecy, silence, and judgment. If you put the same amount of shame in the petri dish and douse it with empathy, it can't survive. . . . Shame is that warm feeling that washes over us, making us feel small, flawed, and never good enough."[7] A close companion that usually accompanies empathy is grace, which is why it is our hero to combat the damaging effects of shame.

(Here's a tip: during interpersonal conflict that leaves you dumbfounded, ask, "What did I do that made you feel small and unwanted?" You will get right to the problem of an "irrational" anger outburst or a cold shoulder.)

Hero: Grace

If shame says, "We are not enough," and makes us feel small and unwanted, then grace does the opposite. Grace says, "We are enough," and makes us feel large and valued. It honors us and causes us to feel accepted and valued no matter what we do.

Jeff VanVonderen, author of *Families Where Grace Is in Place*, describes the benefits of grace: "Capable, creative, contented people of all faith and depth come from families where grace is in place. Isn't that what we all want?" He goes on to say, "God's job is to fix and change. Our job is to depend, serve, and equip. This is the work of grace. And it is more restful than you can imagine."[8]

When we are recipients of grace, we become powerful dispensers of grace to those around us.

Indifference vs. Passion

Villain: Indifference

When working with couples, the first thing we assess is their passion for staying together and creating what they want. We do this by asking two very important questions that are essential in guiding the therapeutic process. The first question is, "On a scale from one to ten (one is low passion and ten is high passion), where are you at in wanting to save your relationship?"

It is not uncommon for one partner to be at six and the other at ten. We find it is impossible to save or heal a relationship if one or both parties aren't at an eight or higher in their desire to save the relationship. Ideally, it is best if both partners are at an eight or higher, and we see good results with this.

But it is next to impossible to heal a relationship if both partners are experiencing indifference to healing the relationship and therapy is merely their "last ditch effort" to save the relationship.

The second question is this: "What is your ideal relationship?"

Both parties need to have a clear picture and answer to this question so we, as therapists, can assist them in the direction they are passionate about going in their relationship. If a partner resists in answering this question, we are unwilling to move forward because their indifference to what they want will sabotage the passion of their partner. As therapists, we depend on passion to save and heal the relationship. When indifference is present, there is nothing we can provide or give to cause the necessary changes in that relationship.

Hero: Passion

The best way to protect your relationship is to enjoy it. You can concentrate your passion on your partner, without allowing your passion to be redirected to another person or other passions, such as work, kids, hobbies, or friends. Passion is very demanding and single focused. It doesn't allow room for other companions.

When your passion becomes redirected, you are in danger of losing your passion for the relationship.

In other words, take delight in what you have, and stay away from comparing or competing with other relationships to keep it alive. Enjoy the life you have been given and take pleasure in your relationship.

Pain vs. Comfort

Villain: Pain

As I (Jenn) write this, I am on a plane returning from a very painful experience. I had the privilege of caring for my dad as he is in the latter stages of pulmonary lung disease. To watch your hero fade away before your eyes is a very painful experience. The powerlessness this brings, combined with the fear of losing your loved one, is overwhelming.

Pain triggers other pain, and it is common to target the ones closest to us. For me, that was Jake. My fuse was short with him as I felt frustration at minor issues, and my responses were exaggerated.

As two therapists, we wisely recognized this as grief and did what we tell our clients to do: we got some help. In working with a skilled and knowledgeable therapist, we were able to manage the pain and navigate through it, even though we could not extinguish it. And none of us are exempt from pain and the ugliness it can bring out in ourselves and others.

Hero: Comfort

As I (Jenn) worked with hospice in treating my dad, I was reminded of the antidote to pain, which is comfort.

When I called them, anxious and tearful, hospice patiently reassured me to breathe and take my time. When I received loving messages and texts from friends and family, I was reassured my pain mattered and I was not forgotten. When I talked to Jake and my kids, I felt grounded and loved as they comforted me and cried with me.

To go through painful experiences is difficult and challenging, but to go through them alone is traumatic. We cannot avoid the Dark

Forests in our lives, but we can comfort each other through them and embrace the process and each other along the way. Holding someone's hand in the Dark Forest is much better than walking it alone. We were designed to comfort each other through painful experiences.

Confusion vs. Peace

Villain: Confusion

This is the most ambiguous villain of all. It slinks quietly up behind you and emotionally hijacks you. Before you know it, you are responding with defenses you didn't even know you had.

One husband, every time he got confused, would just yell obscenities at his wife and stomp out, leaving his wife confused and alone. She never knew when the hair trigger would go off.

When we worked together to have him say, "I'm confused, will you help me understand?" instead of cursing at her, she was able to assist in giving him the answers he needed to alleviate his confusion, thus promoting a safe connection.

In unsafe relationships, confusion is ridiculed, dismissed, and not tolerated. It is not uncommon for people to feel a lot of shame about their confusion because it often doesn't get acknowledged by the individual or accepted by others. Instead of working to create clarity, we fight with each other out of disappointment and confusion, thus creating more confusion and traumatic bonds.

Hero: Peace

The hero to confusion is peace.

Confusion brings chaos, and clarity produces peace.

When we use our energies to create clarity, we bring peace, and peaceful connections allow for loving relationships.

One of the biggest issues in male-female relationships is the misunderstandings about men and women and their unique differences. It is normal to expect your partner to behave like you, but the more we come to understand men and women as having distinct traits, the more we come to understand that they are uniquely created with creative differences.

For example, in our marriage, there are some things we used to fight about that don't irk us anymore since we have come to understand the differences between us. For instance, I (Jake), like many men, do well with adrenaline rushes. I like to drive fast, push myself athletically, and keep a busy schedule. Although Jenn likes to stay active, she needs down time with herself, me, and the family, time to watch "chick flicks," go on walks or dates, have family dinners, and chat.

In the earlier stage of our marriage, it wasn't uncommon for me to stay very busy with work, church, activities, and friends, then squeeze in some time for Jenn or the family. After many conflicts on this, we started recognizing our differences and understanding we each refuel differently. We also learned to talk about our expectations for the day, family visits, vacations, etc., where we both learned to take responsibility for refueling ourselves if our partner was needing something different.

This understanding brought peace and harmony instead of chaos and confusion, which allowed for a healthy connection. It brings more peace to us as a couple when we understand and accept our differences.

Deception vs. Truth

Villain: Deception

One of the saddest things we witness among the couples we work with is when there has been a relationship betrayal caused by deception from one partner.

Betrayal causes anxiety, depression, sadness, and broken trust, and almost always leaves partners wishing they could turn back time and make a better choice for the relationship.

It is one thing to betray the relationship through poor choices, but to continue to lie about it is even more devastating. The confusion mixed with heartbreak is tragic to witness, and recovery from this can only begin with truth.

Hero: Truth

With the introduction of truth, deception dies, and healing can start to take hold. Sometimes people like to give truth in small doses so as to ease the hurt of their partner. Difficult truths that need to be delivered can be compared to an amputation of an arm. To dole out truth in small doses, while a partner continues to question, wonder, and guess which questions to ask, is like amputating the arm, one knuckle, elbow, and section at a time. As one friend puts it in her life motto, "Always give the truth quicker and faster." She lives this, as she consults others and coaches them to become better individuals. She understands that truth really does bring freedom and empowers an individual to be all they can be.

We can be deceived and become our own worst enemy. Just like Adam and Eve in the garden of Eden with the Serpent, this is an age-old problem that has devastating results. According to the Bible, the

Father of Lies prowls around like a roaring lion seeking who he can devour (1 Peter 5:8).

Lies devour the trust, love, and harmony in a relationship. Don't be deceived at the devastating disaster lies bring and the triumphant freedom truth brings.

Rejection vs. Acceptance

Villain: Rejection

This is one of our greatest fears as humans. No matter our age, we will avoid rejection at any cost. As adults, we will go to great lengths to have the right job, clothes, and activities to be accepted by society and "keep up with the Joneses." As teens, we struggle to fit in by wearing the "cool" brands and easily succumb to peer pressure to avoid rejection. As children, we will die without the nurturing acceptance of other humans. It is called a "failure to thrive."

Sometimes we reject one another without meaning to do so because we don't understand what the other person needs to thrive—and what our relationship needs to thrive as well.

We counseled one couple who dealt with this very thing, experiencing a lot of stress and confusion in their home as a result. The wife struggled to be intimate due to a lack of foreplay or intimate romance with her husband. Her husband ignored her needs for peace, romance, and harmony, choosing instead to "grab at her" and expecting her to be intimate when she was exhausted from work or while the kids were playing or fighting loudly in the background.

Instead of seducing her and drawing her to him, he was stressing her out, triggering her sympathetic nervous system, and pushing her away from him.

Unlike many women, she did attempt to teach him what she needed and what was important to her to be intimate, but he rejected her words, needs, and longings. To protect herself, she rejected him, causing a shallow and lonely connection in which both partners felt the devastating experience of rejection.

Hero: Acceptance

When the husband learned to accept his wife instead of rejecting who she was and what she needed, he began to bring romance into the relationship, set up ideal times to connect, and protect her from the stress in the home.

When the wife felt accepted, she felt closer to her husband, who accepted her for who she was and gave her what she needed to be successful sexually. Instead of triggering her sympathetic nervous system, he triggered her love for him. She stopped rejecting him, and they were able to create new patterns of intimacy in their relationship.

Another beautiful story of acceptance came from a woman in a wheelchair. When the wife tapped the side of her wheelchair and told her husband, "You're the only reason I want to be free from this contraption," he kissed her on the forehead and said, "Honey, I don't even see that thing."[9]

We all long for unconditional acceptance, don't we? Indeed, to receive a loving look from a dear one who knows us—flaws and all—and still accepts us is one of life's greatest treasures.

When we're in the Dark Forest, it's easy to get turned around and confused. Sometimes we may think we are "sleeping with the enemy," and in some cases we might be. But in most cases, we are just confused by our own feelings, clouded by our past experiences, and doing our best to move out of the darkness and into the light.

Author Coco Ginger says it best: "In my story, you're the villain. But in my heart, you're still the reigning king."

Keeping your partner in your heart as the reigning king or queen will make all the difference as you navigate through the Dark Forest together.

2. Fight fairly by following the rules.

We just looked at seven villains that can hurt your marriage—and seven heroes that can save it. We can't urge you enough to identify the villains in your relationship, then replace them with the heroes of Love, Grace, Passion, Comfort, Peace, Truth, and Acceptance.

This by itself will help you stop seeing each other as enemies and help you both feel accepted and loved.

And when you *do* have conflict, there are rules that can guide you so the conflict doesn't undermine your sense of safety or throw anyone into solo survival mode.

When our kids were young and we would play games as a family, it was not uncommon for our eldest to slyly change the rules to shift the game to her advantage, as only older siblings can do. My son would get so frustrated and holler out, "Sissy's cheating!" After which the game promptly ended in a torrent of tears as game pieces, along with words and blows, were thrown at each other mercilessly.

Are we not sometimes just grown-up kids? How many times do we manipulate, accuse, blame, lie, and omit the truth to get the "game" to go to our advantage? When we play the game called "conflict," it is critical for us to follow the same rules. Otherwise, the game will end in chaos rather than resolution, and before we know it, we will find ourselves behaving like a three-year-old, throwing words, accusations, and more at our precious partner.

Here are some fair fighting rules to help move you from conflict chaos to conflict resolution:

The Never and Always List

Never:

- Abuse your partner verbally or physically
- Say "I don't love you" or "I want a divorce"
- Threaten the relationship
- Ignore your behavior when you have done a "never" behavior

Always:

- Take turns listening and sharing feelings and needs
- Sit down
- Take time to resolve
- Apologize when you are in the wrong

Time-outs

Time-outs may be needed to get out of the flooded state and avoid sneaker waves. It is normal for conflict to be unproductive or destructive when you are hungry, angry, lonely, or tired (HALT). This is Alcoholics Anonymous's advice to recovering addicts and is applicable to us all. Take time-outs, but remember to take time-ins too. Imagine a basketball game that took a time-out but never resumed the game. It would be frustrating to experience and observe.

Seek resolution and own your part in the conflict. Seek win-win solutions and negotiate a compromise. Assume the best and listen with your heart to your partner. Don't hesitate to solicit the help of an experienced therapist to assist in reaching a place of agreement if you are both struggling to get there on your own. We have benefitted many times from the skill of good therapists, who have helped us reach a place of agreement. John Gottman says that "60% of issues are unsolvable," but many times resolution can emerge from mutual respect, understanding, or an agreement to disagree.

When I (Jenn) worked at a psychiatric hospital for adolescents with a variety of challenging issues, it was not uncommon for there to be conflict among the patients. Part of their treatment was learning how to resolve conflict, so we would set up a conflict resolution meeting. There were three rules they had to follow in order to participate in the meeting, and we would not facilitate it unless both parties agreed to them. These were the rules:

1. Seek to resolve; come with an attitude to resolve.
2. No name calling.
3. Take turns listening/sharing without interrupting.

To this day, I am still amazed at how these young, highly disordered, medicated adolescents could resolve conflict with ease, friendliness, and empathy as they held to these rules. I never remember stopping a meeting because they were not adhering to the rules. And I am reminded that the feeling of being connected, heard, and understood is more valued than the need to win a fight. If they can do it, how much more can we?

3. Fight fairly by exiting quickly.

My (Jenn) ever safety-conscious father would often teach me about keeping myself safe. It was not uncommon for him to sit down at a movie theater and ask me, "Where would you go if there was a fire?" Then he would point out the red exit signs in the theater and instruct me not to panic but to move toward the red blinking light.

In conflict, I've often longed for the red blinking exit sign that could be seen through the smoke and darkness, beckoning me to safety. Just like in a smoky theater or a Dark Forest, the longer you stay, the more at risk you are for getting lost or losing your life. Unproductive, chaotic conflict robs you of the life and love of a relationship and can harden your heart and cause bitterness and resentment to take root. Many times, when our clients realize how much they are hurting themselves and their partner, they are more apt to learn better ways of exiting the darkness and entering into the light.

Here are some techniques to exit the Dark Forest as quickly as possible:

1. Choose a hero, not a villain.
2. Confess what you did to violate connection and peace. Remember and discuss your values and make a plan to honor them.
3. Develop your own exit strategy (humor, jokes, time-outs, dialogue, etc.).

4. Repair what you break or hurt.
5. Do-overs can help erase lots of mistakes.
6. Forgiveness always brings freedom.
7. AAA—Acknowledge, Apologize, Amends.
8. Follow the magic ratio (5:1) for positive to negative comments.

Another thing we like to encourage couples to do is to create an Avalon for your relationship. Avalon was, in Arthurian legend, an island paradise in the western seas to which King Arthur was taken after he was mortally wounded in battle. Metaphorically speaking, this becomes the place you go or the rituals you do after the battle to get out of the Dark Forest. This can be spending time together in the bedroom or on the back patio, a special park, playing, dating, or trips away. This is the time to restore your relationship after it has endured a painful time or season.

Sometimes you need to take something apart to rebuild it in a stronger, more lasting way. Erik Erikson, a well-known psychologist, has said, "A crisis can be a turning point; by making you vulnerable it can heighten your potential for positive change. Sometimes it takes the threat of losing something to make you realize its value. Until you feel compelled to leave, you may not realize you are happy where you are and want to stay."

And always remember: a kingdom divided against itself cannot stand. (Mark 3:24).

REFLECTION

Describe a time when you and your partner resolved a conflict successfully, and what you each did well.

Circle the top two villains that threaten your relationship:

FEAR SHAME INDIFFERENCE PAIN

CONFUSION DECEPTION REJECTION

Create a list of fair-fighting rules for your relationship:

❶

❷

❸

❹

❺

Describe how you can exit a Dark Forest more quickly and with less damage to your relationship.

6

QUEEN SCHOOL

TEACHING THE KING ABOUT HIS QUEEN

Tattered and torn, but not defeated, the prince and princess emerged from the dark forest. Searching for the bright light that drew them out of the woods, they found an old book resting in the grass between some rocks. Its gem-studded cover glimmered and cast brilliant light in all directions. Intrigued, the prince and princess sat down together, opened it, and began to read. As destiny would have it, the ancient book spoke of love, oneness, and how to become a prosperous king and queen. The prince read aloud as the book taught the many great mysteries of a woman's pink kingdom and how to truly know his princess. The humbled prince learned how a king must invest his treasure wisely for his queen's well-being, affirm her beauty, create intimacy, and connect with her innermost desires. Through it all, the prince saw how different they both were yet how perfectly they were made to fit. He discovered what it would take to serve as her hero again.

PART ONE: NAVIGATING QUEEN SCHOOL

Knowledge is power, and the truth will set you free. In this stage of the journey, wise kings have the opportunity to learn what truly inspires and invigorates their queens.

I (Jenn) will be your guide through this chapter, men, as we take a look at the heart longing of your queen—and how you can meet that longing today and throughout the rest of your marriage. We'll also talk about the power of making good investments and what it takes to truly know and appreciate your queen.

Women, feel free to read along, or skip ahead to the next chapter where Jake will be your guide as you navigate King School.

Men, as we navigate Queen School together, we're going to explore three aspects:

- **The Heart Longing** your queen feels most deeply at this destination ("*Know Me!*")
- **The Crisis** that threatens your success *(Not Being Known)*
- **The Key** to meeting this heart longing *(Pay Attention)*

Remember, while each destination has a primary heart longing, these longings won't disappear when you reach the next destination.

These are longings that must continue to be met throughout your entire marriage!

Now, let's dive in.

The Heart Longing: "Know Me!"

One Kingdom is established and maintained when the King not only knows his Queen but appreciates the ways in which she is different from him.

The first thing to grasp is that the heart longing of your queen is this: "Know me!"

Your queen desperately wants to be known by you—not just for how she looks on the outside but for who she is on the inside.

One of my clients was frustrated with her husband, who kept ignoring her and putting his family of origin in front of her. In desperation, she looked up at the ceiling and wailed to anyone who would listen, "I just want him to *know me*!"

Being known helps a woman feel loved and treasured. When you know her, you are able to take her desires, dreams, and needs into account when making choices. She is asking one of life's greatest questions, "How do I matter to you?"

Your woman wants to feel loved, cherished, and captivating, not because she is presenting a flawless façade to you, but for everything she truly is.

After all, Cinderella was loved and wanted as a princess *and* as a peasant. That's a powerful dynamic in this story: if the Prince had married Cinderella on the night of the ball without being introduced to the bigger picture of her life (including the mistreatment she had suffered and her resilience), how emotionally safe could she possibly have felt to him? She might have lived with fears and insecurities that one day he would reject her if he truly knew her.

My point is, when a woman feels truly known, then respected and accepted, barriers to intimacy are dissolved, and she feels loved and cherished by her king.

I want to dispel a myth that leads to a lot of confusion and conflict with couples (and lots of job security for me as a therapist!). One of the most popular myths I encounter in working with my couples is this: "If you love me, then you'll know me."

Women can fall into the trap of thinking that if you truly love them, you'll automatically know them perfectly without them having to actually tell you who they are, what they are thinking, and what they really need.

As you can imagine, this single myth provides endless conflict in relationships.

And it's not very fair to men.

Because men tend to be concrete thinkers, no matter how much you love your woman, you will probably never know her unless she *tells* you who she is! There is no shame in not knowing exactly what your wife needs *if she won't tell you*.

You're not a mind reader.

And you're in good company. For the most part, men have come to the conclusion that understanding women can be daunting.

Not too long ago I was preparing for a business lunch I anticipated would be difficult, and I was stressed out. Jake helped me prepare and comforted me before I went.

When I came home, Jake asked, "How are you doing?"

I said, "Same as this morning." (Code for: If you really love me, you'll know I'm sad and you'll care about how my lunch went and you'll ask about that.)

He said, "Want to go out on the boat?"

"Ohhhh, I guess," I responded. (Which of course was code for: I'm still having a rough time, and maybe soon you'll ask how my lunch went.)

Jake said, "Okay! I'll get the boat ready!"

I was tired and cranky and felt unloved and rejected. As you can imagine, it was not one of our better boating experiences.

Hours later—when we were speaking to each other again—we processed what had happened. I finally told him about my tough lunch experience, and Jake said, in exasperation, "Why didn't you tell me?"

I couldn't answer!

I realized how much time I had wasted trying to bait Jake into showing concern for me, but he never took the bait. It would have been so much simpler if I'd just told him!

Let me give you another example. One woman complained to me her husband never made coffee for her, despite the fact that she had a put on a pot of coffee for him every morning for two years. Then she looked longingly at the ceiling and remarked how she would feel so loved if he did this for her.

I asked her why she didn't simply ask him to do that for her.

She looked at me aghast and said, "If he loved me, he would know what I wanted! If I ask him and he does it for me, then it doesn't count because I had to tell him."

Men, this is called a double bind, and it makes people crazy. Help dispel this myth by telling your woman you love her and you need her help getting to know her, since you have never been a woman and she is your only manual.

Not succeeding in a relationship with your queen can make you feel helplessness and powerlessness in ways that cripple the relationship.

Men have been educating me for more than two decades on how they're wired and how overwhelmed they often feel in relationships. Men are designed to be heroes, princes, kings, and men of nobility, strength, and valor. To operate as anything less can be demoralizing for a man. If they can't feel powerful in the relationship, they will find areas in which they can feel powerful.

In a men's therapy group I was facilitating, one man gave a concrete example of how this dynamic manifested in his life. After describing how helpless and powerless he felt when in conflict with his wife, he added that after a fight he would go to his workbench and sort screws. He felt so overwhelmed because he couldn't please his wife, he had to find a place he felt powerful and stable. He could sort screws with accuracy and efficiency and gain his power and stability back.

The frustration for men in marriage was once best summed up by one of my male clients: "It's like I went from Prince Charming to the Frog Prince."

Men have a tenderness that is not currently being recognized, nurtured, or admired in society. Because of the misunderstandings that often muddle the genders, men are often not recognized or respected for what they need to do to be a woman's Prince Charming.

They are left in a no-win situation and shamed for not being able to figure out how to be successful with their queen.

Similarly, women are often criticized, misunderstood, and judged when they simply long to be known by their men.

Understanding our differences is the first step to accepting and respecting these differences. Why is this so important? Because without mutual understanding, acceptance, and respect, it's impossible to build real relationships full of trust, love, and security.

Here are some interesting facts about the differences between men and women:

- Women bond through secrets; men bond through competition.
- Women have a collaborative, pack-like mentality; men have an individualistic, hierarchy mentality.
- Women across cultures value relationships and benevolence; men value power and achievement.
- Women are attracted to power and seek emotional intimacy as a top need; men are attracted to vulnerability and seek physical connection for intimacy as a top need.
- On average, women speak about twenty thousand words a day; the average man racks up about seven thousand.

Let's take a moment and explore communication further, since how men and women communicate is one of the most distinct differences. Women can hold up to three to four conversations at one time; they can talk and work, are often external processors, and tend to be polite, engaging, and interactive. In other words, they tend to "circle the bush" rather than getting to the point.

Men, on the other hand, often struggle with being able to talk and work at the same time; they are often internal processors. They can be more blunt, direct, less interactive, and get right to the point. When I work with men and communicate like a woman, I often hear, "Just give it to me straight."

In one of our couples' workshops, we like to broaden understanding of the communication differences by having couples build a Play-Doh house together. We instruct them in the importance of working together and working quickly, as they have a time limit.

As they begin the project, we see the man getting right to work quietly building the biggest and best house, while the woman talks as she creates, attempting to work collaboratively only to get silence from her man as he is fully engrossed in his task. The woman often goes from mildly frustrated to quitting all together, as she makes attempt after attempt to get him to collaborate with her verbally while he works. If the man stops working to talk or listen to his queen, he stops working and appears as if he is awakening from a deep sleep.

This doesn't surprise us, since women can talk and work at the same time more easily than men. This is because these skills are centered in opposite sides of the brain, and women's brains have four thousand more neurons connecting the right and left sides of their brain than male brains.

If men understood, accepted, and respected this about women—and women understood, accepted, and respected this about men—a lot of frustration would be avoided.

How does your relationship benefit when your queen feels known, accepted, respected, and appreciated? A woman who feels these things is inspired to be

- **Happier.** This can manifest itself in being more creative, helpful, cheerful, affirming, content in her beauty—and less resentful, depressed, and critical.
- **More secure.** Security is a top need for a woman. When she feels secure, she nests, feels understood, protected, loved, and safe. She produces more of the bonding hormone oxytocin, making her more affectionate, loving, affirming, and sexual—and less adrenaline, which can make her feel restless and irritable.
- **More sexual.** While men can feel anxious and seek pleasure, it's more difficult for women to perform sexually when they are anxious, as these engage two very different parts of the brain.
- **Healthier.** This is due to the increased oxytocin and feeling loved by her king.
- **Stronger.** Feeling known, accepted, respected, and appreciated empowers a woman with the knowledge that she is in a strong, healthy partnership.

You may have heard the sayings "Happy wife equals happy life" or "When mama ain't happy, ain't nobody happy."

Most men want harmony and peace in the home, and they want to be a hero to their wife. This is good for men's self-esteem and self-respect, and it sets the wife up to do what she does best: nurture and love.

The Crisis: Not Being Known

A crisis happens when a king stops getting to know his queen, leaving her feeling unknown, unaccepted, disrespected, and unappreciated.

This happens when he stops getting to know her, stops listening, and is inattentive to her heart.

When I was growing up, sometimes when my mom talked to my dad, he would respond by saying "uh-huh" in that monotone voice many men have perfected, and she would know he wasn't listening to her. To prove her point she'd insert the words "and the monkeys were hanging from the chandeliers," which was my dad's cue to really *listen.*

It's a fun example, but the realities of an "unheard" woman are anything but fun. A woman who feels unknown and unheard can turn into that complaining and nagging person who often says, "You never listen to me!" She can become critical and closed off. She may exude negativity, criticism, nagging, and even depression She may often repeat herself in an effort to be heard.

A tragic example of this is the husband who didn't listen to his wife about her desire to have more babies and got a vasectomy without her knowledge, then coerced her to sell and give away all the baby items.

Eventually he took her to a therapist for marriage counseling because she lacked the desire to be intimate. The therapist blamed her for the failure of the marriage, and she came to me, a severely depressed, emotionally shut-down woman who found herself crying endlessly. Because the husband viewed her to be the problem, he was unwilling to attend therapy, so I had to teach her to listen, assert, and nurture herself so she could be heard.

Women who feel stressed and unheard produce too much adrenaline and not enough of the bonding hormone oxytocin. They become angry, depressed, and resentful of their partner. Misunderstandings are rampant and cause both partners to assume the worst of each other. The low trust manifests an abundance of conflict.

This can further a vicious cycle. Angry over being criticized or not having sex, a husband can lash out at his unheard wife. Both become confused about how to get out of the negative cycle, and the relationship continues to spiral downward.

> Dr. Robert Travis, codirector of Marital and Health Studies at the University of Alabama, lists the most common complaints of husbands and wives:
>
> > WIVES: He doesn't listen to me, he takes me for granted, he's not romantic, and he doesn't help much with the children.
> >
> > HUSBANDS: She doesn't understand that I need time by myself, she nags about little things, she expects too much emotionally, she complains that I spend too much time at work.[10]

It can feel like a daunting challenge for men and women to truly connect. Especially in today's culture. While the role of men may have appeared easier in past generations—just provide financially for the family—today women can provide financially for themselves, so they need men to fulfill a greater role in their lives. Women are seeking provision that goes beyond physical needs, which can be more abstract and difficult for women to communicate—and for men to understand and appreciate.

Which leads to the question, "What can we change?"

According to Sonja Lyubomirsky, author of the book *The How of Happiness,* 50 percent of our happiness is influenced by our genetics, 10 percent by our circumstances, and 40 percent is under our control.[11]

I am going to talk about the 40 percent.

The good news is that controlling your happiness is easier than you think—but there is a cost.

The Key: Pay Attention

The key to knowing your queen is pretty simple when you think about it: just *pay attention.*

You've captured her hand; now capture her heart by learning how to pay attention to her so you can truly know her. And as you do—as you listen to what she needs to thrive—she will feel loved.

Learning how to truly know your queen is an investment in your relationship. You cannot expect to invest two dollars and get a return of $200,000. Similarly, relationships thrive proportionately to the investment. The more you invest, the greater the return. When you truly know your queen, you can then choose to cherish her. In fact, the more you know her, the *better* you will be at cherishing her.

PART TWO:
YOUR QUEST IN QUEEN SCHOOL

I want to give you some practical tips on how you can pay attention to your queen and invest wisely in your marriage.

Here is your mission:

1. Pay attention to the time you invest in her.

Do activities and life with her. One man wanted to go hunting for his vacation time, but his wife wanted him to be with her and the kids. After some negotiating, they came to a compromise and achieved a win-win. They do camping trips together with other families during which the men get to hunt.

What are her favorite colors, foods, clothes, makeup, perfumes, lotions, activities? Occasionally, Jake interrupts a session to bring me what Starbucks affectionately calls the "why bother": a soy, decaf, sugar-free vanilla latte. He is tuned in to my favorites, and he confidently knows what I enjoy drinking. One of my close friend's husband is so good at paying attention to her desires that she has to be careful what she asks for or he'll do whatever he can to get it. I haven't figured out how this is a problem for her yet.

2. Pay attention to your communication.

It is important to differentiate between obeying and listening. You can actively listen to your queen, and it doesn't mean obedience or complying with whatever she's saying. Active listening is affirming, empathetic, and attuned to what your queen is saying. Once listening has taken place, you are both primed and ready to negotiate and collaborate a solution, even if that solution is to agree to disagree amicably.

Affirm her beauty—privately and publicly. My dad passed away after being married to my mother for fifty years. And in those fifty years, he always commented on my mom's beauty in front of us kids and others. There was no room for others to question whether my dad thought my mom was the only one for him. Give compliments for who she is and not for what she can give.

3. Pay attention to emotions.

Your emotional quotient is based on your skills at understanding your emotions and the importance they play in your life.

Occasionally I ask my male clients what value they see in their emotions, and I have never heard an adequate answer. Most men appear to think of their emotions as an unwanted fly buzzing around their heads, and they are more inclined to swat those emotions away instead of embracing and giving value to their feelings.

Here's why emotions are so important: they let us know when we have unmet or met needs. When we can match a feeling up with need that is either being met or not being met, we increase in our EQ.

I often compare men to dragons, with tough, scaly exteriors but soft undersides and hearts vulnerable to being easily pierced. When men are in pain, they often breathe fire, hurting and confusing others. This only adds to the misunderstanding and hurt of men, as women respond by continuing to sting with hurtful words and criticism.

Men, share your feelings and tell your queen when you're hurting. Expose your heart. Get beyond anger and humor to your real feelings.

One couple complained of the husband's excessive anger. They both knew it was a problem. When I asked his wife if she had ever heard him say, "I'm afraid," she said with all sincerity, "He's never afraid."

After some discussion, it was a startling discovery for both to understand that every time he got angry he was afraid, and every time he raged he was terrified. He was afraid of losing power in the relationship and terrified of losing her. As he began talking about his fear (and learned how to take breaks when he did feel angry), his anger began to dissipate. As he courageously talked about his fear of being abandoned because his mother left him at a young age, his wife was able to respond with compassion versus hostility.

Some people have said men have three emotions: anger, rage, and humor (I hope no one actually believes this!). Psychologists say there are seven primary emotions that are culturally universal and develop within the first six months of life. They are surprise, interest, joy, anger, sadness, fear, and disgust.

Learn to expand your emotional language and grow your EQ, or your emotional intelligence.

Ironically, women are experts at identifying emotions, while men are experts at identifying their needs. In other words, women often know what they feel but rarely know what they need, while men often know what they need but rarely know what they feel.

If men can use their energy to listen, affirm, and validate their queen's feelings, they can be of great assistance by helping her move to resolution by helping her identify what she needs.

More About Meeting Her Needs

This means learning to nurture her. When I am busy working, it is comforting when Jake makes me breakfast and brings lunch to me. Many women do this naturally—they are often the ones making meals and caring for the physical needs of the family—but men can learn this as well. Men need to remember to care for the physical needs of their queen, especially when both partners are caring for the financial needs of the home.

One husband came to see me who complained of not getting along with his wife. She was lonely and ready to leave the marriage, and insisted he see me for therapy. He was a wealthy, highly successful farmer and spent twenty minutes talking about his work, how to tend the fields and the equipment, and how to get the best return on his investments.

I complimented his natural ability and skill in farming and nurturing the land to yield a good harvest. Then I asked, "How can you care for your wife like your fields so you can have a good return?"

We talked about getting to know his wife so he could care for his wife's needs. He left inspired, with the concrete challenge of nurturing his wife with the same fervor he used to farm his land.

I think many women relate with the feelings of one of my clients, a woman who had been married for thirty-two years when her husband told her, "Thank you for propping me up all these years."

In confidence, she told me me, "I don't want to prop anyone up anymore." In fact, she resented the fact that he acknowledged her support of him but had never thought of supporting her in return.

When I asked if she had ever told him about her frustration and resentment, she said no.

I asked her what would happen if she told her husband, "I want that back," and encouraged her to give it a try.

She went home and told her husband that she wanted to be propped up, too, and—after all these years—she finally got it. She had never thought of asking for it because of the "if you love me, then you'll know me" myth.

This includes providing for her financially as well as for her wants and needs to the best of your ability and within your values for your life.

The husband of one of my clients spent money on cigarettes, chew, and gambling—but became furious if his wife bought diapers for the baby or a coffee for herself. Since he made most of the money, he controlled the use of the money and bullied her if she tried to spend for the family's needs or her wants.

Another client, married twenty years, had to work three jobs to make ends meet while her husband did nothing to provide for her or the household needs. One of my friends frequently tells her daughter, "Never marry a man who is afraid to work."

In addition, work on increasing oxytocin—the bonding hormone—with your queen through affection, affirmation, partnership, foreplay (at least forty-five minutes!), romance, laughter, deep breathing with her, eye contact, and friendly exchanges.

Help her to organize her emotions by listening to her feelings, helping her identify her needs, and reassuring her when she's stressed. How can you comfort her? Try offering verbal assurances, holding, and hugs.

Well-known theorist Virginia Satir says, "Hugging can be vital for your emotional well-being. Everybody feels skin hunger throughout their lives, and unless that hunger is satisfied by touching, there's a vital void in the emotional make-up that's going to cause deep unhappiness. We all know that babies thrive on frequent stroking. Well, adults are no different. When they are not patted on the hand, embraced around the shoulder or hugged, they withdraw into themselves. I prescribe four hugs a day for survival, eight for maintenance and twelve for growth."[12]

Believe it or not, something as simple as watching chick-flicks together can be bonding and increase her levels of oxytocin.

Here's why this is so important: when oxytocin is flowing within a woman, she is more prone to be sexual. She feels bonded with you—instead of feeling that she needs to keep her guard up with you. Experts say it takes up to ten nonsexual touches per day for a woman to be able to feel open and ready to be touched sexually. But after a couple has been married for many years, it is common for the man to skip those ten nonsexual touches and, in the interest of time and efficiency, go right for the sexual zones. This alarms a woman and causes the hormone of adrenaline to increase in her body, thus causing her to go into fight-or-flight mode when you approach her.

As you can imagine, this is counterproductive for sexual encounters and causes a woman to back off in a protective posture.

Women rarely know what they need sexually, so they react by withdrawing or shutting down, which frustrates the man and complicates their sexual relationship.

One client was ready to leave her husband because she "loved him but was not in love with him." He was devastated! But after exploring the relationship, I could see how they got caught in this negative sexual cycle. The husband had a habit of groping at his wife sexually, causing her to be alarmed and withdrawn sexually. As we worked together to learn how to increase oxytocin, she found herself surprisingly "back in love" with him and desirous of a sexual relationship with him. His patience and skill at getting to know her paid off as he was able to meet her unique needs with love and care.

Kings, I ask you, "How do you have a happy kingdom and a happy queen?" Simply put, rule *together*. Partner with her in helping her rule her kingdom effectively so she can successfully make purple with you. Slow it down. If you want to be *together* with your queen, you'll need to figure out how *to-get-her*!

Know her. Accept her. Respect her. And appreciate her.

Together, you can make beautiful purple.

REFLECTION

What does it truly mean to "know" your queen?

Shade in each of the scales below to rate your current level of investment in the following areas (1 = lowest, 10 = highest):

TIME

1 10

TIME

1 10

EMOTIONAL INTIMACY

1 10

LISTENING

1 10

What does your queen need from you when she feels . . .

excited about a success?

sad about a loss?

hurt from an offense?

QUIZ: What are your queen's favorites?

Food:

Color:

Activity:

Store:

Candy:

Hobby:

Animal:

Destination:

TV Show:

Shoe Size:

7

KING SCHOOL

TEACHING THE QUEEN ABOUT HER KING

Next, the graceful princess took the old, wise book and began to read on. It taught her the many riddles of a man's soul and how to become an honorable queen. She knew that her understanding of the prince's heart was lacking, and she was eager to learn. The book explained man's need to be honored and welcomed, not criticized or dismissed. She read about the great care she must take with her words. The wise book revealed a man's desire to protect and defend and to be valued as the woman's hero. The princess began to realize the deep spirit of conquest that lived within her husband, and her eyes began to sparkle with pride for him as they once had. United in perspective and understanding, the royal couple felt true love's fire rekindle between them once again. Renewed, they traveled on toward their new kingdom.

PART ONE:
NAVIGATING KING SCHOOL

What really drives and awakens men? In this stage of the journey, wise women learn about the power of words to capture the heart and soul of their king. Armed with these insights, queens discover what it means to become an honoring partner.

Women, I (Jake), will be your guide through this chapter as we take a look at the heart longing of your king—and how you can meet that longing today and throughout the rest of your marriage.

As we navigate King School together, we're going to explore three aspects:

- **The Heart Longing** your king feels most deeply at this destination *("Honor Me!")*
- **The Crisis** that threatens your success *(Not Being Honored)*
- **The Key** to meeting this heart longing *(Speak Carefully)*

The Heart Longing: "Honor Me!"

One Kingdom is established and maintained when the queen honors and respects her king and understands his differences. What is your king asking of you at this stage (and others) in your journey together?

Honor me.

Kings long to be honored and respected by the people closest to them. This is true for both men and women, but we men often have an increased awareness and need to feel like we are important and worth respecting. We want to be honored in how we are treated and spoken to, and there is a powerful innate longing in every man to be honored as the provider and protector. There is a reason why our armed forces use the word *honor* in many of their mottos, and when they discharge a soldier from active service, it is called either an honorable or a dishonorable discharge. The desire for honor is reinforced over and over in the military and in everyday society. In fact, one survey found that after surveying hundreds of men and conducting dozens of interviews, most men would choose to feel honored and respected over feeling loved.[13]

Now, let me address the elephant in the room. It's possible that about now you might be thinking, *Wait a minute! Women long to be honored too!*

And I agree with you. Women long to be honored, and many times men unintentionally take advantage of all that women do without giving them the honor and respect they deserve.

One study shows that when couples consist of two spouses working full-time, women still do 70 percent of the household and child-raising duties—in addition to their full-time jobs! This is frustrating and dishonoring for women, especially if they then get criticized for not "putting out" in bed.

This is a maddening position for women. I feel ya! I know what you're after: you crave emotional intimacy, and I know we guys aren't always good at knowing your heart or paying attention to your needs.

But trust me when I say that it's not that because we don't care. In fact, almost every guy I've counseled desperately loves his queen and truly wants to be her hero, her prince charming, and her knight in shining armor—if only he knew how!

One client's wife was going through the grueling process of getting tested to see if she in fact had cancer. She was scared to death and was dreading an upcoming appointment with the doctor. She had told her husband weeks in advance about the appointment so she could get his support through this terrifying process. He promised to be there, but when the morning came for the appointment, as she got up and got ready to go, her husband just kept sleeping. Assuming he had decided not to go with her, she left without him.

The pain of that day created pain in their marriage for years to come.

Eventually the husband ended up in my office. As he told me his story, he introduced me to the phrase "never again moment." The day he allowed his wife to face a terrifying situation alone became that kind of moment for him, and he never missed an important doctor's appointment again.

Jenn can tell you about some of my "never again moments" inspired by the experience of giving her lame gifts or no gifts at all for Christmas or birthdays.

My point is, I understand your need as a woman to feel honored and appreciated, and you deserve to be treated with honor as well.

But right now, you're here to learn how to meet the heart longing of your husband, so let's get back to the task at hand, which is empowering women to honor their kings.

We all know men and women are different and struggle to understand each other. Reinforcing this, Abigail Van Buren said at the top of her list of the ten most common problems she saw in her "Dear Abby" letters was, "My wife doesn't understand me." Men often complain of this same thing in my office when they talk about feeling misunderstood, expected to be or act like their wives.

In an effort to help women gain a better understanding to the world of men, I have compiled a short list of important facts about men:

- Men have a one-track mind . . . not just regarding sex. Men's brains are extremely compartmentalized and much less connected than women's. Men's brains have been described as waffles with all the different compartments, while women's brains are like spaghetti. In fact, research has revealed that men have four thousand fewer neurons connecting the left and right sides of their brain than women. So if the two sides of women's brains are connected by a six-lane interstate, men only have a single-lane dirt road.
- Men are visually stimulated and are extremely sensitive to the female touch.
- Men have been socialized and pressured to discount their feelings. This is where we get the commonly held expectation that "men don't cry."
- Men take words more concretely and literally than women. They will focus on following their

understanding of the words even if they don't make sense.

- Men respond more to actions than words. If a group of men were living as roommates and one of the guys kept leaving his dirty socks on the floor, the other guys in the house would tell him once to keep them picked up or suffer the consequences. Then, when he comes home and finds his socks going up in flames in the backyard, he knows he forgot to pick them up and accepts the results. Actions really do speak louder than words with men.
- Men want sex to feel loved, and women want to feel loved to have sex.
- Men are microwaves and women are crockpots when it comes to sex. When men see their wife naked, they are ready to have sex in thirty seconds flat. Women need to have the love and affection simmering all day to feel emotionally ready to make love.
- Men want to be the hero and save the damsel in distress. Research shows that the male brain is physiologically designed to protect and provide. In fact, this is one of the main reasons why they have historically not allowed women in combat, because men will potentially leave their post, disobey orders, and disrupt the chain of command just to save a woman. We can look to the horrible 2012 movie theater shooting in Aurora, Colorado, to see evidence

> of this. The three boyfriends who sacrificed their lives for their girlfriends became referred to as "The Aurora Three."

The Crisis: Not Being Honored

When the longing for honor is not met in a man, it creates a crisis. Our hidden insecurities come to the surface, and we start to wonder if our character is really that bad to deserve this dishonoring or disrespectful treatment.

The truth is, men are desperate for approval and validation of our manhood and will go to great lengths to prove this.

Not that we may ever admit this to our queens. After all, our culture has set men up to

- stuff their feelings
- never cry
- never ask for help . . . or directions
- get criticized for being like a caveman
- overperform and seek approval

John Eldredge argues that every man asks the question, Am I good enough and do I have what it takes? And when that question does not get answered in the heart of a man, he looks to the woman in his life to answer it.

The tragedy in this is how many men struggle with this insecurity and are desperate to hear from a woman that they are worthy. And when they can't find a woman who can answer the question for them, they can turn to the image of a woman on the screen and fall into the horrible pit of pornography addiction.

In truth, men need to get this question answered by their Creator so they can bring their strength and confidence to their queen.

Men have come to learn to put their armor on. Like a dragon, men are designed to have thick armor—he's built to be a protector, after all—but that dragon still has a soft, vulnerable underbelly. This is his tenderness and insecurity beneath the surface—and why he desperately seeks praise and affirmation. If all he gets is criticism and contempt, he will use his armor to hide behind and protect his heart. Don't make him wear his armor in the castle to defend himself from the one closest to him, his life partner.

And here's a good reason to be careful not to damage him with your words: when a man feels built up and honored, he has more motivation and confidence to love you and meet your needs. If you want to hear his heart, make it safe for him to come out.

A husband once told me about a time when he forgot to get something from the store that his wife had asked for. When he returned home without the item, his wife told him he could no longer be trusted, and called him irresponsible, unreliable, and useless. When she attacked his character, she attacked him at his core, and he felt demoralized and crushed, retreating to his cave to lick his wounds.

When men feel criticized, rejected, and dishonored, this brings out their insecurity and causes them to stop loving their leading lady and to disconnect emotionally. You can easily hurt his ego without realizing it. Men look to their woman for validation, and when they get the opposite, they end up shutting you out to protect their ego.

The Key: Speak Carefully

The key to honoring your king is to *speak carefully.*

Compared to most men, women can appear to be professionals when it comes to using words and talking. Which is why I often say many women are capable of "verbal judo," verbally putting their husbands in a submissive choke hold in sixty seconds flat. Dennis and Barbara Rainey say, "Words are like seeds. Once planted in your mate's life, your words will bring forth flowers or weeds, health or disease, healing or poison. You carry a great responsibility for their use."

Also, as the biblical proverbs tell us . . .

- "Death and life are in the power of the tongue" (Proverbs 18:21 ESV).
- "Gracious words are a honeycomb, sweet to the soul and healing to the bones" (Proverbs 16:24).
- "The words of the reckless pierce like swords, but the tongue of the wise brings healing" (Proverbs 12:18).

At four years old, my son illustrated this best when he said, "When Sissy [his name for his sister] speaks mean to me, it's like knives going into my heart." (For the record, when Sissy heard this, she was immediately moved to tears and quickly apologized.)

Research shows that words do in fact hurt. Ridicule, disdain, humiliation, taunting, etc. all cause injury and inflict lasting physical effects on brain structure. It has also been proven that words can affect our mood in both directions, to lift it up or tear it down.[14]

PART TWO: YOUR QUEST IN KING SCHOOL

I want to give you some practical tips on how you can honor your king by speaking carefully. Here is your mission:

1. Speak carefully by affirming your king.

Men thrive on positive affirmation and encouragement. This literally becomes his fuel to love. How did you get his attention in the first place? By telling him how strong, talented, and valiant he is. We long to get that affirmation from the woman we love.

This is why when a man cleans the bathroom once a year, he expects his wife to invite the neighbors over and throw an appreciation party while women roll their eyes and say, "Oh brother, I do this every week!" (I've actually been known to tell women that men need a "Scooby snack" of affirmation when they do a "trick" you want them to repeat.)

Words are life-giving or life-stealing. Your husband may have physical power, but you have power in your words. You can use that power for good or evil. Interestingly, the Disney movie *The Little Mermaid* revealed a profound truth when Ariel lost her voice and was stripped of her power, being forced to woo her prince without the power of her words.

A woman seeking counsel from Dr. George W. Crane, the psychologist, confided that she hated her husband and intended to divorce him.

"I want to hurt him all I can," she declared firmly.

"Well, in that case," said Dr. Crane, "I advise you to start showering him with compliments. When you have become indispensable to him, when he thinks you love him devotedly, then start the divorce action. That is the way to hurt him."

Some months later the wife returned to report that all was going well. She had followed the suggested course.

"Good," said Dr. Crane. "Now's the time to file for divorce."

"Divorce!' the woman said indignantly. "Never. I love my husband dearly!"[15]

This woman's plan backfired (although with great results!). I'm guessing that after she built him up for all that time, he responded so positively to the affirmation that he began behaving like the man of her dreams. This is yet another example of the incredible power of words.

Want another example of the power of words? Positive words actually have a positive impact on our bodies as well as our emotions. Researchers have discovered that people who are constantly bombarded with positive words (instead of negative words) actually have stronger muscles. I'll bet you didn't realize you could have the power to get a buffer husband out of this deal!

A while back my wife shared a dream with me in which there were two boxes. During the dream it was revealed to her that all the negative things she ever said to me were in the negative box, while all the positive things were in the positive box. In her dream, she opened the negative box and dumped out the contents—and realized how overwhelmed she would feel if she were on the receiving end of all those negative comments.

I distinctly remember the morning after that dream getting lots and lots of affection and affirmation from her.

Make sure you are putting far more in the positive box than in the negative box. Masters in relationships tell couples to shoot for the magic ratio of five to one—five positive comments for every negative comment. I encourage you to do the same for your husband by using your words to inspire, nurture, validate, appreciate, affirm, encourage, and express gratitude.

If you're not sure where to start, here are a few ideas:

- Invite him to be your hero by affirming his character. Call out the qualities of nobility in him: courage, patience, integrity, justice, and mercy.
- Be careful not to attack his character when you are frustrated with his behavior. Even though he will mess up many times, he still needs your grace and honor (this by no means condones any type of abuse or domestic violence).
- Since our culture puts a huge emphasis on a man's responsibility to provide for his family, make sure to honor and affirm him for his efforts in providing. When he is hearing lots of praise and affirmation, he will seek you out to hear more, which is the best way to get more quality time with him.
- Lastly, you can also affirm him by showing interest in what interests him. According to research by Willard Harley, one of the top things men need from their partner is for them to be a recreational companion.

- Not surprisingly, Harley also revealed that sex is the top need for men, so you will not go wrong when you initiate to meet this need of his.

2. Speak carefully when he is not there.

If you practice honoring your husband when he is not around, it will be easier to do so when you are together. There is an epidemic of husband bashing in America, and many wives are more than happy to join you in putting down their husband and yours. Decide not to be one of them.

It will mean the world to your husband when you find ways to show him how proud you are of him. Instead of keeping a mental list of gripes about your husband, keep a mental list of affirming, positive things about your husband, and share these things with others when the opportunity arises.

It is said that one of the best ways to show value to someone is to talk positively about them to someone else so they can overhear. In fact, that is what we are taught to do with kids also . . . and we men are just little boys grown big.

Not only do men want to give their hearts to you, but they are hardwired to give their lives for you. Enrique Iglesias speaks for your man the best when he sings, "Let me be your hero."

Remember to use your power with words and speak carefully by affirming your king even when he's not there.

3. Speak carefully in how you express your needs.

You need to realize men are taught—and our culture reinforces this idea—that their needs are super important. This means that your husband might not intuitively think about your needs.

In addition to training men to be takers, our culture and society also trains women to be givers. This creates inequity among the two of you and does not inherently encourage oneness.

If you haven't figured this out already, hinting, nagging, and criticizing to get your needs met doesn't work. Most women tell me they don't want to be the nag but can end up unintentionally going there anyway. The downside of nagging is that it not only doesn't work but also can have negative repercussions. Men are competitive and like to win, so if your husband feels like he is consistently failing at making you happy, his impulse will not be to keep trying and failing but to quit and do something else at which he can experience success. Jenn mentioned an example of a client who would retreat to his workshop where he could (successfully!) sort screws rather than interact with his wife and feel like a failure. This is a perfect example.

And yet your needs are just as important as his. It's important for you to realize and embrace this fact. In fact, it will be hard to honor him if you don't honor yourself by valuing your own needs enough to address them with your husband.

So if nagging doesn't work, what does?

Just because your husband loves you doesn't always mean he knows *how* to love you. Where do you think your husband or partner would have learned how to love and nurture a woman? From his father? Grandfather? The media? Not likely. He desperately needs you to teach him how to fill your love tank.

Invite your husband to meet your needs instead of criticizing him for not meeting them. Use your words to teach and educate him, not to shame and belittle. He can't read your mind, so say what you mean and mean what you say.

Another thing, women, I encourage you not to take all the stupid things your king tends to do too personally, because this is not a true reflection of how much he loves you.

I would also encourage you not to ask why he is doing or not doing a certain thing, especially when you already know the answer or know that he doesn't know. He will need time to have an answer to your question, and it is okay to hold him to this. Bottom line, men struggle to read emotional cues and are often accessing a different part of their brain. A recent study showed that men took twice as long to read women's emotions than men's due to them having no personal reference point. When you need to disconnect temporarily, make sure you tell him why. Men are extremely cause-and-effect oriented. Also remember, men are very concrete and logical, so when life goes on as normal even when your needs are not being met, men assume all is good in the castle. The kindest thing you can do for your husband is tell him why you are not being drawn to him and what you are needing to change that. There is nothing worse for men, when they initiate sex, than hearing you have a headache, when it's really that your needs are unmet. If all he gets is rejection, he doesn't automatically connect the dots that it is connected to your unmet needs.

Remember, men understand actions more than words. Don't be afraid to put your needs in writing and draw a diagram if necessary; you can't make the assumption he knows. If you want to be loved and your needs met, speak carefully in how you express your needs.

REFLECTION

What does it truly mean to honor your king?

Rate how carefully you speak to your king overall (circle one):

1	2	3	4	5	6	7	8	9	10
Worst									Best

Circle your top two needs from the list below; then briefly describe how well you communicate these needs to your partner:

Comfort
Attention
Time
Affection
Conversation
Security
Intimacy

What are some practical ways you can speak more carefully to your king?

List some of your favorite qualities about your king.

8

GARDEN OF LOVE

The noble couple happened upon a blissful garden, lush with tall grass, trees, and a cool brook that trickled softly. A tapestry of bright colors adorned the greenery throughout this serene landscape. The prince and princess decided this was a perfect place to rest and refresh. The garden was still and peaceful, full of open space, warm sun, and light breeze. The pair needed this time to reconnect and give their full attention to one another. It was as if all their walls had finally come down, and they could be fully transparent and vulnerable once again. Laughing and reminiscing over stories of their romance, their friendship was deepening. Fear, shame, and pride melted away as trust and assurance took their place. The noble pair experienced oneness that they could not have imagined. They were learning to love fearlessly. Now, only their final destination lay before them.

PART ONE
NAVIGATING THE GARDEN OF LOVE

Michael Ende, author of *The Neverending Story*, says, "There are many kinds of joy, but they all lead to one: the joy to be loved."

Love is our greatest desire. We desperately seek it, often sacrificing much in our attempts to achieve it. In fact, the universal quest of most fairy tales is to acquire true love.

When we love and are loved by another, our experience can be compared to Adam and Eve's in the garden of Eden, where the first couple inhabited the earth, void of fear, death, and shame. Just as the garden of Eden was a beautiful, harmonious space, when you and your spouse reach the Garden of Love in your journey, you'll find yourselves enjoying more peace and serenity than at any point on your journey so far.

And although life in the Garden of Love is not attainable every day, it is a bit of heaven on Earth where a couple can enjoy a secure, loving space.

As we navigate the Garden of Love together, we're going to explore these three aspects:

- **The Heart Longing** felt most deeply at this destination *("Love Me!")*
- **The Crisis** that threatens your success *(Not Being Loved)*
- **The Key** to meeting this heart longing *(Get Naked)*

Remember, while each destination has a primary heart longing, these longings won't disappear when you reach the next destination. These are longings that must continue to be met throughout your entire marriage!

Now, let's dive in.

The Heart Longing: "Love Me!"

One Kingdom is established and maintained when the king and queen learn the significance and power of love. The heart longing of this destination is "Love me!"

When we feel loved, a lot of good things happen. We stop wrestling with the fears of rejection, abandonment, death, hurt, pain. We feel secure, bonded, and attached. When a couple has no fear of abandonment or betrayal, they enjoy a deeper love, where trust is high and playfulness, humor, and friendship abide.

Giving and receiving love is, indeed, our deepest longing and desire.

And love has other benefits too. For example, it is the most powerful motivator in heaven and on Earth.

West Point teaches, "The best predictor of strong leadership is the ability to give and receive love."

General Patton demonstrated this well, as he held the admiration and love of his army and told them often he loved them. He publicly affirmed and celebrated what they did for the rest of the army and was able to accomplish great feats with his army.

Love is the primary motivator in battle. It is what makes the impossible possible.

Historians attributed the success of the American Revolution to the deep love the people had for their newfound country, and their passion in fighting for it showed. Equipped with axes, rakes, and knives, the Americans took on the greatest known military at that time, the British Army and Royal Navy, and soundly defeated them.

It is an honor and privilege to love deeply and fiercely and to be a person with great love.

So love is our deepest desire.

It is the most potent motivator.

And here's something else that love can do: love creates measurable, physical benefits in the brain and body of the beloved. When we feel loved, we reap these benefits:

- Less active stress glands
- An increase in the DHEA hormone that acts as a stress buster
- An anti-cancer effect (married folks have a lower rate of cancer than singles)
- Fewer headaches and less back pain
- Better blood circulation
- Longer life expectancy
- Lower blood pressure
- Reduced risk of heart disease
- Faster healing

Love has also been proven to be an effective pain anesthetic.

James Coan, a neuroscientist at the University of Virginia, conducted experiments in 2006 during which he delivered a small electric shock to the ankles of one group of subjects: women in happy, committed relationships. Tests registered their anxiety before and pain level during the shocks. The experiment was repeated, this time while the women held the hands of their partners. This time, the same level of electricity produced a significantly lower neural response throughout the brain. When researchers conducted the same test on women in troubled relationships, however, this protective effect didn't occur.

In other words, if you're in a healthy relationship, the mere act of holding your partner's hand is enough to lower your blood pressure, ease your response to stress, improve your health, and soften physical pain.

Through love, we actually alter each other's physiology and neural functions.

The Crisis: Not Being Loved

The opposite of giving and receiving love is living protected and disconnected from each other. Couples who are living defensively and disconnected hide their hearts from one another and spend their energy on surviving instead of thriving.

When we live defensively and disconnected, our spouse feels a powerful emotion: they feel rejected. Oh, that might not be our intent, but that doesn't change what our spouse experiences.

Let's talk for a moment about the ramifications of the emotion of rejection.

Not feeling loved causes failure to thrive. As we mentioned in an earlier chapter, when babies are not loved and touched, they fail to thrive and, in fact, typically do not survive more than three years. We're not babies, but we still need loving, physical touch, and when we don't get it, our marriages not only fail to thrive but the longevity of the marriage is threatened.

Not feeling loved also causes *physical* pain. In fact, rejection causes activity in the pain centers of the brain that can be measured. In one study, researchers recruited college students who'd just been rejected by their sweethearts. As the students looked at photos of their ex-boyfriends and ex-girlfriends, researchers conducted MRIs and discovered that the insular cortex, the part of the brain that experiences physical pain, became very active.

"People came out of the machine crying," Dr. Lucy Brown said. "We won't be doing that experiment again for a long time."[16]

The body doesn't know the difference between physical pain and emotional pain. It is no coincidence that an image of a heart broken in two is symbolic of emotional rejection in cultures everywhere.

Not feeling loved is also linked with overeating and other addictions. And no wonder! Food is often associated with love, so when love is lacking, people often try to fill that void with overeating. We've often wondered if teaching people how to give and receive love would be more effective than many diets! One woman, married thirty years, whose husband rejected her after having an affair with a younger woman, said with honest exasperation, "I just can't stop eating!" Other addictions, such as work, sex, drugs, alcohol, media, and more, are also used to fill the love void.

Not feeling loved makes it difficult to love ourselves and others. The beast in *Beauty and the Beast* had a challenging time loving others since he looked on himself with such disdain and disgust. Then Belle came along. Her love for him helped him see himself in a new light.

In Matthew 22:39, the Bible says, "Love your neighbor as yourself." Not loving yourself makes it hard to love your neighbor, which translates in Greek as "near one." As we counsel couples, if we see one or both partners are hampered by insecurity or self-loathing, we tell them, "This is a luxury your marriage can't afford."

It is very difficult to give and receive love when you don't love yourself. You cannot give what you don't have. It's imperative and crucial to give and receive love, but we can't do that if we are hiding behind fear and shame.

The Key: Get Naked

The key to loving your partner in the Garden of Love is this: get naked.

Getting naked brings us back to the very first fairy tale in the garden of Eden. When we're as naked as Adam and Eve were in the dawn of creation, we are real and vulnerable. We're not hiding or protecting anything—not even our hearts!

Most important, we feel no shame.

The Bible says about Adam and Eve in the Garden, they were "both naked, and they felt no shame" (Genesis 2:25 NIV).

First, let's take a look at shame.

- Shame says, "You're not enough."
- Shame causes you to hide behind fig leaves, or cover yourself.
- Shame produces fear-based behavior.
- Shame is hopeless and focuses on the past.
- Shame is confused about your sense of self and is too busy helping you hide for you to discover or develop who you really are.
- Shame causes low self-esteem and the devaluing of your authentic self.
- Shame cultivates confusion and chaos.
- Shame makes you critical and judgmental of yourself and others.
- Shame is embarrassed.
- Shame hates self and others.
- Shame thrives in secrets, lies, and deceit.
- Shame breeds addiction.

The opposite of shame is not perfection. It's not the absence of mistakes. It's grace.

- Grace says, "You're enough."
- Grace doesn't hide behind fig leaves.
- Grace produces love-based behavior.

- Grace is hopeful and focuses on the present and future.
- Grace has a clear sense of self and lives in acceptance with a high self-esteem and value for your authentic self.
- Grace cultivates peace and clarity.
- Grace embodies acceptance and encouragement.
- Grace is confident.
- Grace loves self and others.
- Grace has no secrets, is honest, authentic, and transparent.
- Grace breeds healthy living.
- Grace communicates, "You are not the mistake and you are okay."

Fear is a close relative of shame. When someone has experienced betrayal, abuse, or abandonment (and at some level, haven't we all?), it's not uncommon to have a fear of intimacy and to struggle to attach to others due to fear.

When fear and shame creep in, we follow the example of Adam and Eve, hiding behind fig leaves, blaming each other ("But God, the woman you gave me made me do it!"), robbing ourselves of giving and receiving true love. And as we know from Adam and Eve's story, shame not only impacts our relationship with ourselves and each other, it impacts intimacy in our relationship with God.

In our work, we often deal with shame coming from the following three areas: addictions, abuse (emotional, spiritual, sexual, physical), and acting out (believing one thing and doing another). When we are able to assist in the healing process, it is a beautiful experience to see the shame dissipate.

Shame is often the result of things done to us and not by us. According to social scientist Jane Middelton-Moz, shame is a common emotional response in adult children of alcoholic parents as well as in those who grew up with depressed parents, abuse, religious abuse, war, cultural oppression, poverty, or parent or sibling death. It is also not uncommon for children to feel shame when their parents' divorce. All these experiences cause an individual to feel vulnerable, helpless, and shamed.

But as common—and even as understandable—as shame may be, there is a tremendous cost. The other common emotion that often comes with shame is fear. Fear chokes out love, fuels shame, and is the antithesis of love.

Men and women have differences when it comes to fear and shame. While women deal with shame through introversion and self-hatred, males express their shame through anger and violence. Women feel fear stronger, and men feel shame stronger. In a study, both were asked what would be the worst thing about being homeless and losing your job? Women were far more concerned for their safety and living on the streets, while men were far more concerned about failing in life as providers than about their personal safety.

Whether male or female, handling fear and shame inappropriately or abnormally plays an important role in causing many troubling issues, such as social phobias, eating disorders, domestic violence, substance abuse, road rage, schoolyard and workplace rampages, sexual offenses, and a host of other personal and social problems.

PART TWO:
YOUR QUEST IN THE GARDEN OF LOVE

The key to addressing fear and shame is *get naked*. We're going to explain more about what mean by that in a moment. We will also explain your mission.

But first, we want to add this about fear and shame.

Addressing fear and shame can be done through a variety of methods, including inner child work, therapy, group work, prayer, readings, meditation, and other avenues of healing.

People you can talk to about your feelings of shame or fear include your spouse, God, groups, friends, family, therapist, religious leader, and other safe individuals who will accept you.

Practicing "grace talk"—with others and with yourself—is also powerful. Shame language says, "You should have . . . ," "If only you were more . . . ," "How could you?" or "You're not enough." Grace language says, "You're okay," "You're not damaged goods," "I love you anyway," and "You are enough."

This story is a beautiful illustration of the difference between "shame talk" and "grace talk." A couple, married for fifteen years, began having more than usual disagreements. They wanted to make their marriage work and agreed to try an idea suggested by the wife. For one month they planned to drop slips of paper in a "Fault Box" for each other. The boxes would provide a place to let the other know about daily irritations. The wife was diligent in her efforts and approach: "leaving the top off the jelly jar," "wet towels on the bathroom floor," "dirty socks not in hamper," on and on until the end of the month.

After dinner at the end of the month, they exchanged boxes. The husband reflected on what he had done wrong all month. Then the wife opened her box and began reading. They were all the same: the message on each slip was, "I love you!" When we are focused on expressing grace and love to our partner, it's easy to overlook the faults and magnify the love.

This husband showed grace to his wife. Can you apply this kind of grace and "grace talk" to your spouse?

Perhaps a more challenging question is, can you apply it to yourself? Strengthening your true self with grace-filled self-talk is one of the best ways to ward off shame. If you know who you are and what your strengths and weaknesses are, and have lovingly accepted yourself, it will help you develop more shame resistance and shame resilience.

When it comes to fear, there is a verse in the Bible that sheds light on what we can do: "Perfect love casts out all fear" (1 John 4:18 ESV). The Bible also tells us that "God is love" (1 John 4:8). In other words, where God is, there is perfect love. To conquer fear, we suggest couples learn to relate to a loving God. Ask Him to provide love in your heart for your partner and your relationship as a powerful reminder that we don't have to do this on our own. We can call upon the "Great Magician" in our fairy tale to give us the added "magic" to make our fairy-tale experience the coveted "true love" of every fairy tale.

In addition to asking for help from God, here are some other ways to address fear:

- Acknowledging what you are afraid of to yourself and your partner.
- Acquiring help, new information, resources, and spiritual guidance.
- Loving deeply, starting with yourself. You cannot give what you don't have. When you love deeply and securely, you operate from a different part of your brain. Your body responds differently, and you are able to bond out of love versus fear.

Because fear and shame of any kind thrive in secrecy, exposing it is often a first step in the healing process.

Ready to get naked? Great. Here is your mission:

1. Get naked with your play.

There are several ways to play with your partner:

- Recreational activities, such as sports, outdoor activities, and games
- Social activities with your partner and others
- Sexual activities, such as romance, affection, foreplay, intercourse, etc.
- Rituals, such as daily gym time, coffee dates, weekly church, etc.

As men and women, it is also no surprise we play differently. Men marry for a recreational partner, while women marry for a best friend. Men often bond in their play through competition, while women bond in their play through collaboration and emotional connectedness. Just the differences in play, if not understood and respected, can have disastrous results when a couple goes to play. Regardless of the differences, we all need play to have healthy, fulfilling lives.

Modern technology reveals that play lights up the brain in such desired areas as clarity and memory. Common sense tells us that if we've been encouraged to play as a child, it comes more naturally as an adult. Conversely, psychiatrist Stuart Brown's research suggests that the absence of play in early life can have dire consequences. In fact, he claims, most serial killers were deprived of childhood play.[17]

Since play is so critical to the development of an individual and a relationship, it is no surprise that couples who stop playing together stop thriving together. When working with couples, it is not uncommon that couples who are in distress have stopped playing or dating each other. One of the first things we do is get the couple playing together so we can build a trusting, safe foundation essential for solving conflict.

Because the couple is so used to bonding through fighting, we give them the challenge to go on a date without bringing up any issues. We stress the importance of this so much that we have them charge each other a dollar if they do or discuss anything unpleasant. (We actually got this idea from our marriage therapist when we were having more conflict than play, and it worked beautifully for us, so we have passed it on to our couples.) This usually brings out the good-natured competition in both, and they set about dating with the intent of creating play in their relationship.

Play changes the state of the marriage, builds a fondness toward each other, and sets the stage for one of the most intimate forms of communication: laughter. Like a yawn, laughter is contagious and has quite a few benefits. Below is a list of what laughter does:

- Reduces stress and tension
- Stimulates the immune system
- Increases natural painkillers in the blood
- Decreases systemic inflammation
- Reduces blood pressure
- Lifts your spirits
- Brings couples closer together
- Creates freshness in the relationship

When laughter fades, so does the love and the bond, and the couple begins to bond out of fear and shame instead.

Surprisingly, sex is not the most important part of a love relationship. A Syracuse University survey asked married couples to rank the ten most important things in a marriage relationship. Caring came in first, a sense of humor came in second, and communication came in third. Sex came in ninth, just ahead of sharing household duties.[18]

When we stop laughing, we are working too much, getting imbalanced, and the conflict increases. Take it from these professionals: Bob Hope described laughter as an "instant vacation," and Jay Leno says, "You can't stay mad at somebody who makes you laugh." Laughter is what gives resilience to our relationships and perspective to our fights.

2. Get Naked with your Pain

Fairy tales and many popular Disney stories are familiar with pain and loss, and often make a powerful connection around some sort of pain, loss, or crisis. It becomes the quest of the main characters to resolve their crisis, heal their hurts, and mourn their losses. Consider these examples:

- Ariel wanting legs in *The Little Mermaid*
- Pinocchio wanting to be a real boy
- Dumbo losing his mother in a tragic way
- Belle having to live at the castle with the beast away from her loving home
- Nemo losing his father and home
- Bambi losing her mother
- Rapunzel living in solitary confinement with just her hair to keep her company

Thankfully, there arrives a hero on the scene, often with some sort of magical influence, who helps the main character recover their loss and have a new life, free from the loss that encumbered them. Someone or something appears that makes their loss appear more bearable and eases the sadness for the viewer. It is not uncommon for a sidekick to bring humor to help aid in their quest, comfort their loss, and befriend them through their tragedy. Look at these examples of sidekicks:

- Nemo has Dori.
- Snow White has the seven dwarfs.
- Belle has the enchanted castle.
- Ariel has Sebastian.
- Pinocchio has Jiminy Cricket.
- Peter Pan has Tinker Bell.

Like the fairy-tale characters, we need a sidekick, a partner who befriends us and helps us cope with the pain and loss life brings, or the pain can be overwhelming to bear. One woman bravely blogged, "Today marks the ten-year anniversary of the day when I slapped my husband and screamed at him remorselessly for not letting me in the bathroom after we ate breakfast. That moment also marks the positive turning point in my battle with Bulimia. I think he saved my life that day."[19]

Move toward the pain and share your pain with one another. Stay with one another and comfort each other through the pain. It is difficult to go through pain, but it is traumatic to go through it alone. Disney understood this well, as he often provided a relief for the viewer when his characters endured challenging losses and tragedies.

Comfort is the antidote to pain. When we hurt each other, it is not uncommon for us to avoid one another or pretend that the hurt is gone. This is because it is much more difficult to listen to the hurt we caused our treasured partner. When we hurt one another, it takes a courageous individual to stick around to validate, accept, and comfort the hurt we brought to our partner.

It's even more surprising when they still desire our comfort. One husband had an affair, but the wife still wanted to be held by him and reassured of his love for her. Comfort doesn't make the deed go away; it helps to heal the hurt the deed caused.

When we don't comfort each other, it raises concerns and questions in the eyes of those watching. We wonder at the lack of empathy, as comforting a loved one demonstrates love, care, empathy, and concern.

At the royal wedding of Prince Albert of Monaco and Princess Charlene in 2011, the media questioned the tears of the princess and the lack of comfort by her prince. It was described as a bittersweet wedding.

The emotional part was their time at the Chapel of Saint Devota where she symbolically laid her wedding bouquet. In that moment, the emotions overwhelmed Princess Charlene to the point of sobs. The hearts of viewers broke for her. We wanted to reach out and hug her—because her prince certainly wasn't doing that. Some media sources described him as looking annoyed—*really* annoyed. As his new—as in twenty-minutes-new—wife sobbed, some demonstration of comfort—an arm around her, a pat of her hand—would have endeared him a thousand fold to his people. Instead, he looked as if he couldn't have cared less.

Comfort not only soothes the one in discomfort, but it soothes others observing the story. We were made to give and receive comfort at a time when our hurts are unveiled. It reminds us we are all human and restores hope during the most desperate of times. Some of the most endearing pictures of war, a hellish experience on Earth, are a soldier carrying a bloody child to safety, two soldiers comforting each other in their last hours, or a friendship forged with a local villager. These are the pictures that make such horrors manageable to viewers and decrease the amount of trauma to the participants and the viewers.

When we are hurting, we're not always pretty. We can actually display very off-putting and in some instances dangerous behavior. But through it all, we are saying, "I need you to care for me."

One teacher understood this well. On a Tuesday morning in March of 2006, another school tragedy almost occurred in Nevada when a fourteen-year-old student walked into Pine Middle School, pulled out his parents' .38 pistol, and opened fire. The young man squeezed off three shots, hitting one boy in the arm and striking a young girl with a ricochet (both victims recovered). One teacher, Jencie Fagan, walked right up to him, put her arms around him in a hug, and told him she wouldn't leave him. He dropped the gun, and Fagan held him firmly against her until other teachers arrived to help. Fagan later said that she believed anyone else would've done the same, saying, "I look at the students as if they're my own."[20]

Comfort with tears is a recipe for healing. Tears of joy are also a way to express profound emotion. There is a video circulating on social media of people who break down in sobs when they get their new puppy. It is moving and sacred to see these individuals so overcome with joy, they can only fall to the ground in tears as they snuggle their precious gift.

3. Get naked with your personal lives.

We are shocked in working with our couples how few partners are aware of the personal lives of their significant other. It is not uncommon for each partner to have low awareness of the finances, social connections, and emotions of their partner. We encourage spouses to be knowledgeable and revealing in the following areas:

- Finances – be aware of the money in the bank, credit card balances, and spending.
- Phones – share passwords, questionable texts, and social media, viewing your partner as a friend who can help protect your character.
- Friends – know your partner's secret or unknown friends.
- Computers – when it comes to email, games, and messages, share passwords and be transparent in your exchanges.

Are you ready to enjoy life full of love and grace and without fear and shame? Then truly love each other by shedding the shame and getting naked in your play, pain, and personal lives.

Sow seeds of love and grace so you can harvest the fruits of love and grace.

Plant seeds of grace and love, not weeds of fear and shame that choke out your garden of love.

And learn from others doing this well. Sometimes we approach older couples who appear in love and ask them what their secret is. We've heard a variety of answers, but one of our favorites is from a Middle Eastern man married forty-two years who says his key to success is that he never calls his wife by the term *wife*, but always refers to her as his "friend." He explained, "When I call her *friend*, I treat her better, like I would one of my dearest, most cherished friends."

In your spouse, you have been divinely provided with a friend who can make the pains of life bearable through the expression of love in all its wonderful aspects. Cherish one another, and express gratitude to God and each other for your partnership, for life is not meant to be lived alone.

REFLECTION

Describe a season in your relationship when you felt the most loved.

How have fear and shame hindered your ability to love and to be loved?

Being as specific as possible, what would grow in your relationship if more grace and love were present?

How naked, or transparent, is your relationship overall? (circle one):

1	2	3	4	5	6	7	8	9	10
Hidden									Naked

In what ways can you be more naked in the following areas:

Play

Pain

Personal Life

9

ROYAL CASTLE

Finally, the newly crowned king and queen arrived at their royal castle. It was a magnificent place fit for a fairy tale. The grand castle—draped in their beloved royal purple—stood majestically in the center of their kingdom. Deeply inspired by their journey, the king and queen were determined to rule together in unity, and to protect and treasure the oneness they had built. They recounted their experiences: the early romance of their young love, peril in the dark forest, and their ultimate victory and peace. Without this great adventure the royal couple knew that their kingdom would not have been possible. Filled with inspiration and vision, they committed to leave a legacy of greatness that would impact and benefit others. While their journey may have ended, another was just beginning. The king and queen were ready for the trials and blessings to come, confident that together they would prosper. And so, not a love like theirs could be found throughout all the land. Once and for all, they lived happily ever after.

PART ONE: NAVIGATING THE ROYAL CASTLE

It never ceases to amaze us how inspired and moved we feel as we watch imaginary, animated characters do inspiring things. We find ourselves wanting to cheer for them and stand up and applaud when they have accomplished the seemingly impossible. For example, when

- Prince Charming finds Cinderella by trying her shoe on all the women in the kingdom
- Nemo is reunited with his anxious yet loving father
- Ariel gets true love's kiss with Prince Eric, recovers her voice, finds her legs, and gets a whole new life with the man of her dreams
- Belle gets her prince, no longer hidden by his beastly nature

We often tell our couples how inspiring they are to us as they face their pain and challenges, all in the hope of making a better and greater relationship. These are some of the bravest heroes to us.

Within every one of us reside these longings: to be inspired to accomplish great things, to experience resiliency through loss, and to recover wonder, joy, and hope.

As we navigate the Royal Castle together, we're going to explore three aspects:

- **The Heart Longing** felt most deeply at this destination *("Inspire Me!")*
- **The Crisis** that threatens your success *(Not Being Inspired)*
- **The Key** to meeting this heart longing *(Rule as One)*

Remember, while each destination has a primary heart longing, these longings won't disappear when you reach this final destination. These are longings that must continue to be met throughout your entire marriage!

Now, let's dive in.

The Heart Longing: "Inspire Me!"

Everyone wants to be inspired by greatness and be an inspiration to others.

There is something in us that longs to live and experience greatness—and also be remembered for the greatness we've achieved. We crave being recognized for achieving the impossible and being remembered for the exceptional.

Feats of bravery, nobility, and chivalry are carried down through stories and writings. We cheer for the hero who beats all odds, saves the damsel in distress, and defeats the villain. We create Halls of Fame, MVPs, and Oscar Awards to celebrate achieving the exceptional. Works of art and beauty are invaluable treasures, cherished through the centuries. Buildings such as skyscrapers, pyramids, and bridges speak of the engineering greatness that inspires architects and engineers today. Amazing athletes beat all odds to win the gold medal.

We can hear the song, "Fame, I'm gonna live forever!" echoing in the hearts of all.[21] We deeply desire to be inspired by greatness so we can live and leave our greatness to be remembered for others. This is an innate human desire.

As part of this desire, we also long to inspire our children to do great things and inspire others. We want to be proud of the contribution we gave this world through them. In reaching our greatest potential, we also inspire our children to aim high, thus rendering an upward mobility toward success.

Chicago architect Daniel Burnham said "Make no little plans; they have no magic to stir men's blood and probably themselves will not be realized. Make big plans, aim high in hope and work. Remember that our kids and grandkids are going to do things that would stagger us."

In our lives and practices, we have been inspired by the concept of Peer Marriage, where parenting and financial provision for the family is shared between spouses.

Today this model has a name, but when we envisioned it, we didn't know how to live it practically or what it might be called. We just knew how we wanted to live. In order to move forward in our vision, we were inspired and instructed by another couple living a similar model.

After a beautiful, honest conversation with them, we were able to emulate what we loved about their family life.

Inspiration calls us to a different way of thinking and living, and fuels us with the hope of living better lives, creating better things, and leaving a hopeful legacy for our children.

The Crisis: Not Being Inspired

A crisis happens when we are not inspired: we do not produce great works, actions, accomplishments. A disinterested, boring, dreary, nonadventurous cloud takes over our life. In fact, when inspiration, greatness, and creativity are missing from our lives, the void is so great that we sometimes look to false substitutes and destructive things to fill the space. We can begin to idolize people, who end up falling, leaving us discouraged and angry at the betrayal of being disappointed.

When we stop living our unique greatness, we stop inspiring others—including our partner. When we stop living our greatness and therefore stop being an inspiration to those around us, we stop inviting our spouse to live the adventure that we started when our relationship began. When couples stop being an inspiration to one another, the magic goes away. Spouses can start to get bored and look elsewhere for their inspiration. When a couple loses inspiration for the impact they want to have, they get confused, discouraged, and lost.

The way to keep the adventure alive is to continue living your greatness—and continue inspiring each other and those around you to live *their* greatness and leave a lasting impact.

When spouses stop inspiring each other, they

- Stop being adventurous and playing together
- Stop making purple
- Resort to color bullying by wrestling for individual power (blue or pink)

- Fight unfairly
- Stop paying attention to her
- Stop speaking carefully to him
- Stop getting naked with one another

One of the most inspiring things to us is when we see a couple ruling successfully together as one. When they respect one another and draw from each other's strengths in tenderness, love, humor, and courage, they join together to become more powerful. With the rate of divorce on the rise, seeing longevity in marriage is becoming increasingly rare, but seeing a long, happy marriage is inspiring to observe and a wonder to behold.

The Key: Rule as One

There is nothing inspiring about a divided kingdom. In fact, a kingdom divided against itself cannot stand.

When we see marriages with a lot of inequity in power or support, we typically see a lot of resentment, conflict, depression, and hostility. God did not create man or woman to be powerless. God created us with free will, and when we cannot exercise and experience freedom, this creates depression, anxiety, and a host of other issues.

Writer and animator Joe Murray said, "Marriage should be a duet—when one sings, the other claps." Support one another in your dreams and achievements. Rule your kingdom or marriage together as one with equity of power and position.

In other words, the key to keeping each other inspired and excited about life and marriage is to keep making purple.

PART TWO:
YOUR QUEST AT THE ROYAL CASTLE

Are you ready to inspire each other by ruling as one in a purple kingdom of your making? Here is your three-part mission:

1. Rule as one by living as king and queen.

How do you do that? Make purple by creating a beautiful balance and combining your strengths. Come together to nurture your strengths so you can leave a powerful legacy. If you haven't already, give yourselves a promotion from prince and princess to reigning king and queen of your castle. You've earned it, so enjoy being corulers of your kingdom as you create your One Kingdom fairy tale.

When a wife was asked in therapy if she wanted to be her husband's princess, she responded emphatically, "No! I want to be his queen!"

In her marriage, she had been "demoted" below her mother-in-law and was not too pleased about having lived this way for twelve long years. She was fed up with the unwelcomed demotion and demanded her rightful place as queen.

Strive to create in your marriage the roles of king and queen rather than master and slave, king and peasant, or queen and serf. And in your roles, serve each other as every great leader does to make a healthy kingdom. Great leaders are servant leaders and use their power and influence to serve the people.

As Jimmy Evans, pastor and founder of MarriageToday (currently XO Marriage), says, "The best marriage in the world is two servants in love. The worst marriage in the world is two masters in love."

Just like it is difficult to rule a kingdom you never live in, it is difficult to create your One Kingdom when you never leave your kingdom of origin to create a new kingdom. It is important to leave your parents and cling to the one you want to create your new kingdom with. Let nothing come between you as you cling together, coruling your kingdom.

> During his courtship with a young woman named Julia Dent, Ulysses S. Grant took her out for a buggy ride. Coming to a flooded creek spanned by a flimsy bridge, Grant assured Julia that it was safe to cross. "Don't be frightened," he said. "I'll look after you." "Well," replied Julia, "I shall cling to you whatever happens."
>
> True to her word, she clung tightly to Grant's arm as they drove safely across. Grant drove on in thoughtful silence for a few minutes, then cleared his throat and said, "Julia, you said back there that you would cling to me whatever happened. Would you like to cling to me for the rest of our lives?" She would, and they were married in August 1848.[22]

Leaving our families, clinging to one another, and claiming oneness while still maintaining our own identity: this is the ultimate fairy tale. It's a fairy tale complete with villains, a Dark Forest, and supernatural "magic"—our creator God who empowers us to achieve our greatest dreams and make the impossible possible.

When we die, our lives don't end—they begin! What we do here on Earth counts for eternity, so live a marriage you can be proud of in eternity and take comfort in the fact that whatever ails you in your marriage on Earth will not ail you in heaven. If we believe that God created the concept of oneness with our partner, then we need to strategize how to rule effectively together.

2. Rule as one by protecting what you've built.

As in any kingdom, the castle symbolizes protection, strength, boundaries, and safety. When the castle is taken, the kingdom has been infiltrated and most likely overrun. In other words, what good is a beautiful kingdom and a spectacular castle if you don't have anything in place to protect it?

A castle typically has several modes of defense: 1) the moat, which is a water-filled trench protecting the castle's ramparts; 2) the stockade, which is the castle's first line of defense and made up of a row of pickets or boards to keep invaders at bay; 3) the keep, which is the castle's main tower and serves as a final stronghold in the event of attack; 4) the rampart, which is a thick wall that forms the castle's outer defense.

When we have something sacred, we build a defense system to protect it. On a Hawaiian vacation, we visited the City of Refuge, which was built for the sole purpose of protecting Hawaiians who found themselves fearing for their lives after committing a crime. The city had a handmade wall that was seventeen feet thick and made of stones fit together so tightly they needed no mortar. It was inspiring to see what great lengths they went to protect the sacred grounds and the inhabitants who sought refuge there, protected from their victims' family members who sought to kill them before they were able to stand trial.

Protect from invaders.

Marriages and relationships are precious, sacred, and worthy of our most advanced protection methods. We are responsible to protect what we're building and have built, and we are only as strong as our weakest link. In your oneness, develop boundaries and safeguards to keep your relationship safe and free from invaders.

Today we see remnants and complete structures of awesome castles that have been standing for hundreds of years, and it is awe inspiring to think of the great lengths the builders took to protect what was inside. There is nothing more inspiring than your partner advocating for the protection and success of your marriage, and nothing as disheartening as when your partner lets the walls drop, allowing invaders inside. When you let the walls of your castle get breached, you're not protecting what you've taken years to build. Protection is a tenet of nurturance and is needed for something to be safe and grow healthy.

Recognize threats to your kingdom. The truth is, many partners have naively stepped out on their marriage because they didn't maintain the boundaries necessary to protect the marriage. Another factor can be ignorance of how genders differ in feeling aroused and pursued. Women tend to be sexually aroused when a man connects with them emotionally, while men tend to be sexually aroused when they connect physically with a woman.

One of our clients hung his head dejectedly while describing how an affair started through friendly chatting on Facebook and texting.

He enjoyed the friendship and connection. What he didn't realize is that the woman he was chatting with was sexually aroused through the emotional connection. She became emotionally attached and proclaimed her love for him. Taken off guard and feeling responsible for what he had started with her, he participated in a one-night stand that left him and his marriage in ruins.

To restore the health of his marriage and the trust of his wife, he had to set new boundaries. It is important to set boundaries so you are able to play, love, and live together, ruling your kingdom in safety. Establish boundaries regarding who comes into the home, marriage, and life. Be careful who you give your attention to in your mind, heart, and actions. Refrain from obsessive or addictive behavior that keeps you detached from your partner, allowing a breach in your castle and kingdom. Learn to be content and take pleasure in your partner and your partnership.

When asked on his fiftieth wedding anniversary for his rule for marital bliss and longevity, Henry Ford gave sage advice: "Just the same as in the automobile business, stick to one model."

Help each other create a strong sense of security as you protect what you built with commitment and faithfulness.

Protect your time together.

When you were dating, spending time together on the phone, through letters, texting, or dates was easy. Nothing else would command as much time and attention as the one your heart loved.

When we were engaged, Jake had taken a position in Oregon, while Jenn was finishing up her teaching degree in Southern California. Every month, we spent hundreds of hours and dollars (remember when long-distance calls cost a small fortune?) on the phone talking about our days and when we would be together again. When we did see each other, we spent as much time together as we could.

At our wedding, it is no wonder we sang the song to each other, "I'm Thankful We Don't Have to Say Goodbye." Studies show that working couples spend only about twelve minutes a day talking with each other. About thirty-six minutes a day is spent together in cooking, cleaning, shopping, paying bills, and demonstrating affection.[23] If we want to grow something great, we must invest significant time into it.

3. Rule as one by leaving a shared legacy.

Consider this text from one lover to another: "I want it All… I want the pointless bickering, the long walks, the late night phone calls, the good morning texts. I want cute pictures with you, hold your hand, to make food for you, to call you baby. The joking, the wrestling, the fights, the long how I feel text after we makeup. I want to be one of those inseparable bestfriend couple that people are like 'you're still together?' That's what I want."[24]

This sounds like the recipe that fairy tales are made of. All the good, bad, and ugly rolled up in one beautiful mess. Create and tell your fairy-tale adventure, and have fun recapping your resilient adventure. It will be a great story to tell your children and grandchildren, and your story may be able to inspire other young couples struggling to get much past the Hills of Pursuit in their own adventure. Be proud of your harrowing adventure, and remember that *you* get to write the script after the wedding carriage rides off into the sunset.

This is your story, so plan the future chapters of your fairy tale—and remember that this is about living and fulfilling your purpose together.

After all, your marriage isn't just about the two of you. It's about leaving a legacy and making an impact on others.

At this stage in the journey, many couples are finished with the shared task of raising children and often have nothing else to pursue as partners. There is a proverb that says, "For lack of vision or inspiration the people perish." We say, "For lack of vision or inspiration the *marriage* perishes." Don't let yourselves get to this stage and have nothing to pursue together.

You also don't have to wait till the kids are gone to live a life of play, purpose, and togetherness. Your kids need to be inspired beyond themselves too. As mentioned earlier, one of the most treasured experiences we had as a family was taking a trip with the World Help organization to Guatemala.

All year we had saved with the kids to contribute our earnings to the "well fund," which would be used to provide clean water to villages desperately in need. While in Guatemala, we had the privilege of formally dedicating the well we saved all year to see built. We were able to visit some of the poorest regions of the country, and our kids got to feed malnourished orphans taking residence in the local garbage dump. We were able to love the elderly in the local retirement home, and rock the sick, abandoned babies who had been rescued from the mountain villages. Our hearts were full from the experience, and we came home with a renewed vision to provide aid and clean water to those in need for years to come.

Americans love happy endings! You have the power, freedom, and control to write your ending and create whatever legacy you want your relationship to leave. "Happily ever after" doesn't happen just because you fall in love and marry. You must be deliberate about the ending to your love story and the legacy you want to leave.

REFLECTION

Take a moment together and write your Royal Decree. This proclamation 1) states how you intend to rule in unity with your partner; 2) describes how you will protect what you've built; 3) expresses ways you intend to inspire your partner; 4) declares the legacy you desire to leave.

Our One Kingdom Royal Decree

1)

2)

3)

4)

X _______________________ X _______________________

Each of your signatures goes here.

Our Final Charge . . .

You did it! Congratulations on completing TWO CROWNS ONE KINGDOM! In celebration of what you've learned, we encourage you to make some new vows with your partner as a result of reading this book. In fact, if your partner is available right now, turn toward each other, take each other's hands, and make a royal declaration to each other of these One Kingdom vows:

I will choose you by creating adventure.
I will appreciate you by making purple.
I will protect you by fighting fairly.
I will know you by paying attention.
I will honor you by speaking carefully.
I will love you by getting naked.
I will inspire you by ruling as one.

Hans Christian Anderson said, "Life itself is the most wonderful fairy tale of all."

Fairy tales are not just for children. At every age, we crave the adventure of true love and overcoming life's challenges with a committed partner and community of people who believe in us.

We were made for stories and made to live these stories in relationship. Our hope is that you choose to embrace your own real-life fairy tale, complete with adventures, dark forests, heroes, and villains. We long for you and your true love to emerge together from your story as better people and partners and, in the process, for you to weave a grand fairy tale that gets passed on through the words and lives of your family for generations.

This is the heart of marriage: to live a real adventure story that inspires, challenges, and intrigues all who hear it. These are the best fairy tales, and you have the distinct privilege to create your own. And as you tell your story to your children's children, may those magical words "Once upon a time . . . " fill their imaginations with thoughts of magical adventures full of wonder, fright, awe, and love.

This is your fairy tale. Write it, live it, tell it, and don't shrink back from the dark forest moments. They provide beautiful contrast to your quest for true love.

Thanks so much for reading *Two Crowns, One Kingdom.* Our hope is that you will live out your fairy tale with courage, rule your One Kingdom in harmony with your beloved, and live happily ever after!

NOTES

1 "Eating Disorder Statistics," ANAD.org, National Association of Anorexia Nervosa and Associated Disorders, accessed December 3, 2021, https://anad.org/education-and-awareness/about-eating-disorders/eating-disorders-statistics/.

2 "Masaru Emoto – Water Experiments," YouTube.com, November 17, 2012, https://www.youtube.com/watch?v=1qQUFvufXp4.

3 Dr. Charles F. Asked, *Homemade*, vol. 11, no. 7, https://www.sermoncentral.com/sermon-illustrations/26980/carlyle-had-a-very-devoted-wife-who-sacrificed-by-sermon-central.

4 Sarah Bessey, *Jesus Feminist: An Invitation to Revisit the Bible's View of Women* (New York: Simon and Schuster, 2013), 170.

5 Kent Crockett, *The 911 Handbook* (Peabody, MA: Hendrickson Publishers, 2003), 86.

6 Allan Findlay, "Reduce Rear and Shame to Become Closer in Marriage," EzineArticles.com, February 23, 2009, http://EzineArticles.com/2027844.

7 Brené Brown, "Listening to Shame," Ted Talk, Ted.com, March 2012, https://www.ted.com/talks/brene_brown_listening_to_shame?language=en.

8 Jeff VanVonderen, *Families Where Grace Is in Place: Building a Home Free of Manipulation, Legalism, and Shame* (Bloomington, MN: Bethany House, 1992), 14.

9 Marc Chernoff, "101 Short Stories That Will Leave You Smiling, Crying and Thinking," accessed December 15, 2021, https://www.marcandangel.com/2010/12/27/101-short-stories-that-will-leave-you-smiling-crying-and-thinking/.

10 "Common Complaints of Spouses," Bible.org, originally from *Fathergame*, March 1985, accessed December 16, 2021, https://bible.org/illustration/common-complaints-spouses.

11 Sonja Lyubomirsky, *The How of Happiness: A Scientific Approach to Getting the Life You Want* (New York: Penguin, 2007), 116.

12 Virginia Satir, "Good for Emotional Well-Being," originally from *Homemade*, March 1990, accessed December 16, 2021, https://bible.org/illustration/good-emotional-well-being.

13 Theresa, "What Men Need Most from the Woman They Love," Shaunti.com, May 2, 2013, https://shaunti.com/2013/05/what-men-need-most-from-the-woman-they-love-2/.

14 R. Douglas Fields, "Sticks and Stones—Hurtful Words Damage the Brain," rdouglasfields.com, October 30, 2010, https://rdouglasfields.com/2010/10/30/sticks-and-stones-hurtful-words-damage-the-brain/.

15 "Crane, the Psychologist Counsels a Wife," originally from *Bits and Pieces*, August 22, 1991, https://www.family-times.net/illustration/Love/200161/.

16 Elizabeth Cohen, "Loving with All Your Brain," CNN.com, February 15, 2007, http://edition.cnn.com/2007/HEALTH/02/14/love.science/index.html.

17 Michael Sigman, "The Importance of Play: It's More Than Just Fun and Games," HuffPost.com, February 11, 2011, updated November 17, 2011, http://www.huffingtonpost.com/michael-sigman/play-importance_b_821238.html.

18 Thomas Lickona, "Sex," originally in *Homemade*, January 1985, accessed December 16, 2021, http://www.sermonillustrations.com/a-z/s/sex.htm.

19 Bedeempled Brain, "Found another gem of a story.. another sachet of goodness," Facebook, November 10, 2012, https://www.facebook.com/BedeempledBrain/posts/490813917615590.

20 "'Hero' Teacher Stopped Shootoing with Hug," A News, March 16, 2006, http://abcnews.go.com/GMA/story?id=1732518&page=1#.UFeq4qTyb1s.

21 "Fame," written by Dean Pitchford and Michael Gore, Universal Music Publishing Group, Sony/ATV Music Publishing LLC, 1980,

Lyrics.com, STANDS4 LLC, 2021, accessed December 16, 2021, https://www.lyrics.com/lyric/5974275/Irene+Cara.

22 "A Love for the Word," WomensMinistryConnection.com, September 3, 2012, https://womensministryconnection.com/2012/09/a-love-for-the-word.html.

23 "Marriage," SermonIllustrations.com, from "American Demographics," reported in *Homemade*, December 1988, accessed December 16, 2021, http://www.sermonillustrations.com/a-z/m/marriage.htm.

24 _Lost_In_Love_, "I want it All… I want the pointless bickering," iFunny.com post, May 30, 2016, accessed December 16, 2021, https://ifunny.co/picture/i-want-the-pointless-bickering-the-long-walks-the-late-I5NpfNku3.

ABOUT THE AUTHORS

Drs. Jake and Jenn grew up in Southern California and married after becoming college sweethearts and receiving their undergraduate degrees at Azusa Pacific University. Jake and Jenn are both licensed independent clinical social workers with master's degrees in social work from Walla Walla University and have counseled individuals and couples for over twenty years. They received their doctorates in leadership and global perspectives from George Fox University, where they traveled to fourteen countries studying leadership. Out of honor for one another and each other's family, both Jake and Jenn, along with their kids, incorporated each other's last name into their own: Dean-Hill. Currently, Jake and Jenn operate their own private practice as both individual and marriage and family therapists as well as their Corporate Leadership Counseling business. They also enjoy public speaking and conducting seminars on marriage, leadership, and personal growth.

Jake is an avid golfer, and Jenn enjoys expressing her artistic design talent through décor, music, and writing. They have been married almost three decades, and together they raised their two great kids, McKenna and Dawson, in Richland, Washington. As a family, they enjoy warm, sunny days boating on the river or spending time at their beach house in Lincoln City, Oregon.

CPSIA information can be obtained
at www.ICGtesting.com
Printed in the USA
BVHW031817090422
633500BV00006B/14

9 781955 043083